CULTURAL TRADITIONS IN
NORTHERN IRELAND

Previous conferences published in this series have included:

Varieties of Irishness, 1989
Varieties of Britishness, 1990
All Europeans Now? 1991
Varieties of Scottishness, 1997

The illustration facing pages 3, 47 and 91 is *Chez les Sinclairs*, 1956, by Basil Ràkòczy (1908–79) whose father was Hungarian and mother Irish. He worked in London, Paris and Dublin, with frequent visits to other European countries. The painting is reproduced by kind permission of the Trustees of the National Museums and Galleries of Northern Ireland and Mme Jacqueline Robinson.

Cultural Traditions in Northern Ireland

Cultural Diversity in Contemporary Europe

Proceedings of the Cultural Traditions Group Conference
1997

Edited by Maurna Crozier and Richard Froggatt

The Institute of Irish Studies
The Queen's University of Belfast

First published in 1998
The Institute of Irish Studies
The Queen's University of Belfast

This book has received support from the Cultural Diversity Programme of the Community Relations Council which aims to encourage acceptance and understanding of cultural diversity. The views expressed do not necessarily reflect those of the Northern Ireland Community Relations Council.

The extract from 'After the Fire' on p. 62 is reproduced by kind permission of Blackstaff Press and the estate of John Hewitt.

British Library Cataloguing-in-Publication Data.
A catalogue record for this book is available from the British Library.

ISBN 0 85389 720 4

Typeset in Baskerville

Printed by W. & G. Baird Ltd, Antrim, Northern Ireland

CONTENTS

**The Contribution of the Arts, Language and Museums to Cultural
Diversity**

CONTRIBUTORS

Elizabeth Armour is an Inspector with the Department of Education for Northern Ireland.

Jonathan Bardon, historian and teacher, is Chairman of the Community Relations Council.

Jerzy Chmiel is President of the Polish section of the CIEFF.

Paddy Coulter is Director of the International Broadcasting Trust.

John Darby is Professor of Ethnic Studies at the University of Ulster.

Donnell Deeny QC is a former Chairman of the Arts Council of Northern Ireland.

Will Glendinning, former schoolteacher and politician, is Director of the Community Relations Council.

Maurice Hayes, formerly the Ombudsman for Northern Ireland, is Chairman of the Ireland Funds Advisory Committee and Chairman of Trustees of the Mater Infirmorum Hospital.

Eilean Hooper-Greenhill is Head of the Department of Museum Studies at the University of Leicester.

Brian Kennedy is Head of Fine and Applied Arts at the Ulster Museum.

Peter Leuprecht is Deputy Secretary General of the Council of Europe.

Peter Logue is Education Officer for Channel 4 Schools.

Declan McGonagle is Director of the Irish Museum of Modern Art.

Michael McGowan is Chief Producer of the BBC Northern Ireland Education Unit.

Vivien McIver is Staff Inspector at the Department of Education for Northern Ireland.

Sean Nolan, Conference Chairman, is the Chairman of the Cultural Diversity Group of the Community Relations Council, Northern Ireland.

Malachi O'Doherty is a freelance journalist and film-maker.

Marian O'Doherty is Project Officer of Channel 4 Schools' 'Speak Your Piece' project.

Dónall Ó Riagáin is Secretary General of the European Bureau for Lesser Used Languages.

Cesare Onestini is Administrator in the Directorate-General for Education, Training and Youth (XXII) of the European Commission.

Ewa Repsch is Chief Inspector in the Ministry of National Education in Poland.

Alan Smith is Senior Research Fellow in the School of Education, University of Ulster.

Tomislav Sola is Professor of Museology at the University of Zagreb.

John Van Santen is Director of the Artists and Craftspeople in Education Project at the International Centre for Intercultural Studies, University of London.

INTRODUCTION

A decade ago very few would have predicted the direction and the extra-ordinary rate of change in Europe following the revolution in Romania, the dismantling of the Berlin Wall and the rapid break-up of the Soviet monolith. Millions came to enjoy a new-found freedom which cleared the way for an open society and representative democracy. At the same time, the disintegration of old centralised power structures allowed long-dormant ethnic rivalries to gush to the surface in the Balkans and elsewhere in eastern and central Europe. Some began to draw uncomfortable parallels between the nature of the civil war in Bosnia and that of the Northern Ireland Troubles, the longest-running conflict in Europe since the Second World War. As the European Union increased in size, with the promise of peace and co-operation, so the realisation grew that issues of cultural diversity would have to be addressed.

The international conference recorded in the following pages provided a unique opportunity to meet, listen to, question and debate with those at many levels involved in dealing with divided societies across Europe. Participants were able to weigh up and draw upon strategies devised for different reasons and varied circumstances. The European Union objectives for promoting and embedding cultural diversity were considered, and participants will have the opportunity to examine the effectiveness of efforts to put these policies into practice.

All Europeans have much to learn from attempts to come to terms with diversity. Northern Ireland, because of its protracted conflict, has been learning longer than most other regions and has much hard-won experience to pass on. Participants were able to assess the effectiveness of various approaches adopted by voluntary agencies, statutory bodies and by government in Northern Ireland through study visits which gave some practical illustration of how cultural differences might be explored – or even celebrated. Participants enjoyed contact and dialogue with people experienced in cultural diversity; they gained insight into the appli-

cation of good practice and were able to explore how some opportunities for legitimising diversity and accommodating difference have been
taken. It is hoped that these opportunities for the participants might be
enhanced by this record of papers delivered to the conference.

Jonathan Bardon

CULTURAL DIVERSITY: SETTING THE SCENE

APPROACHES TO CULTURAL DIVERSITY IN NORTHERN IRELAND

John Darby

Thirty years ago, when everything seemed more simple and more optimistic, two Americans called Simpson and Yinger listed five possible policies by which a stronger ethnic group could deal with its opponents. They were:

1. assimilation, either (a) forced or (b) voluntary;
2. pluralism;
3. population transfer, either (a) forced or (b) voluntary;
4. continued subjugation;
5. extermination.[1]

You may baulk a little at the cool progression towards the unacceptable, but if you think we have progressed beyond the more brutal options, just think of Bosnia, Rwanda and Burundi during the last few years. But it does help to put Northern Ireland's experience into a broader context.

The management of difference in Northern Ireland

Since the Plantation of Ulster in the early 17th century, the most preferred model of control in Ireland was continued subjugation, not extermination. In the earlier decades, this applied to Presbyterians as well as Catholics, and there is a strong case that the partition of Ireland and the creation of Northern Ireland in 1921 was an unashamed attempt to maintain a system of majority control. Few serious scholars would deny that the first 50 years of Northern Ireland's history were marked by gerrymandering, electoral manipulation and economic discrimination. The search for new approaches may have started before the Civil Rights campaign in the late 1960s, but there is little room for doubt that it was the growth of violence in the early 1970s which sparked off the search for fresh approaches. It continues today.

During the 1970s, social policies, like political policies, were loosely based on the hope that Northern Ireland had a large, untapped middle ground between unionism and nationalism, and that this 'silent majority' needed to be given confidence to make itself heard. Proportional Representation was introduced for local elections in an attempt to fragment the unionist and nationalist blocs. Support was provided for moderate voices, including the mainstream churches and such reconciliation bodies as the Corrymeela Community. By the early 1980s, however, the persistence of sectarian politics and violence raised questions about whether the middle ground alone could deliver an acceptable settlement.

The alternative approach was to accept that Northern Ireland had two traditions with different but equally legitimate cultures and aspirations. Consequently, both traditions should be encouraged to express their cultural separateness without embarrassment. The long-term aim was the evolution of a plural society which accommodated and respected differences. A number of changes, many of them conceded reluctantly after considerable pressure, signalled this shift in policy: the introduction of 100 per cent financial support for Catholic schools; the granting of financial support from government for Irish-language schools; the acceptance by the authorities of Irish-language street signs for some areas; increased financial support for social celebrations, festivals and activities which had traditionally been supported by either Catholics or Protestants; and a new social role for the arts and for museums. In 1988 the Cultural Traditions Group was established with government support to encourage the process. A Community Relations Council was set up to co-ordinate and encourage those working on the ground.

Let me illustrate the shift in policy by focusing on education, the theatre for the most visible changes. I have already mentioned the gradual acceptance and eventual funding of Irish-language schools. But the major reforms concerned the segregation of Protestant and Catholic schools. In the early 1970s there was general concern that there might be a connection between segregated schooling and community conflict. The concern was based on two basic hypotheses: the 'cultural hypothesis' – that segregated schools present children with two very different views of their cultural environment; and the 'social hypothesis' that, regardless of whether or not the two sets of schools are similar or different, the fact of separation encourages mutual ignorance and entrenches hostilities. Underpinning both hypotheses is the suggestion that a higher level of contact between Protestants and Catholics would contribute to an amelioration of the conflict.

These arguments have influenced educational policy and practice in two main ways. The first emerged from a small but growing public demand for the establishment of religiously integrated schools where Catholic and Protestant pupils could be educated together. Public opinion polls during the 1970s consistently indicated that a high proportion of the population claimed to support the principle of integrated education. The first integrated schools opened in the late 1970s. Government support was lukewarm, and most of the integrated schools which opened during the 1980s started outside the education system with the support of funds from private foundations. Public funding was only granted when schools had proven their viability. By the late 1980s government policy had shifted towards a more active support for integrated schools. The 1989 Education Reform (NI) Order finally accepted integrated schools as an integral sector within Northern Ireland's public education system – indeed, some would argue, an advantaged sector. By the end of 1996 32 integrated schools had been established.

The second set of changes in official policy on schooling addressed the experiences of the 98 per cent of pupils educated within de facto Catholic or Protestant schools. It is now required by law that all elementary school pupils are introduced to the concepts of cultural diversity and Education for Mutual Understanding (EMU) within the curriculum. Doubts still remain about how effective the implementation of these directives has been.

These new approaches to cultural diversity – educational and general – did not spring from a vacuum. The last two decades have also seen major changes in the fields of fair employment, equal opportunity, and electoral procedures. Sometimes it is difficult for those working in the eye of the storm to recognise change taking place around them. So how can progress, or regression, be measured in a durable conflict like Northern Ireland's? One way is to imagine the last two decades through a series of freeze-frame photographs. The foregrounds would capture the highlights: internment in 1971, Bloody Sunday in 1972, the 1981 hunger strikes, the war memorial bomb in Enniskillen in 1987, the ceasefires. A more careful study would show that the background has been subtly changing. Northern Ireland is now a more fair society, and this change has been achieved gradually, almost imperceptibly.

A number of serious problems remain, among them the religious composition of the police force, the continuation of emergency legislation and the continuing higher Catholic unemployment rates; the shadow of the marching season shows how far there is still to go. But significant changes have taken place. Some of the more blatant discriminatory practices have been removed many years ago. Franchise abuses were ended by 1969. The allocation of housing – a major issue at the start of the Troubles – has effectively been removed from the roster of grievances. All schools, including Catholic schools, are now funded on a completely equal basis. The employment differential between Catholics and Protestants has been substantially reduced, although there are still bitter disputes about the extent of the improvement. There is no longer an officially sanctioned system of discrimination. The principle of political, social and cultural parity is now accepted much more widely.

The freeze-frame photographs reveal the importance of what might be called the drag effect. As protagonists find new areas for disagreement they often tacitly move towards resolutions of previous sticking points. Agreements are dragged along in the wake of change, the real advance taking place behind the lines, concealed by the sound and fury at the new battle front. The signs of the drag effect are those issues which aroused passion in the past but which are now quietly accepted. An example: in the debate before the 1989 Fair Employment Act, employers strongly opposed the requirement to monitor the religion of their workforces. They argued that workers would defy any attempt to record their religious affiliation. Mass conversions to Islam or Buddhism were forecast, to ridicule the new requirement. They were wrong. In 1989 only 64 per cent of Catholics and 42 per cent of Protestants accepted the need to monitor. By 1993 these figures had risen to 91 per cent and 64 per cent respectively. Religious monitoring had become part of the social scenery.

A number of other fiercely-defended positions are now similarly accepted: the principle of fair employment, and fair access to housing; equal funding for all schools; the inability of either the IRA or the British Army to win a military victory; the Dublin government's involvement in negotiations; the need for endorsement of any political agreement by a majority within Northern Ireland. These may appear undramatic or obvious to younger people. Thirty years ago these principles were at the very centre of political dispute.

Have attitudes changed to keep pace with these developments?

There is still a substantial body of evidence indicating that Catholics and Protestants in Northern Ireland perceive themselves as belonging to distinctive groups, and perceive the conflict to be rooted in the distinction. In some respects 25 years of violence have reinforced the differences. Demographic segregation between Catholics and Protestants has increased. Some families have moved to live among their co-religionists, either in the face of direct threats or from fear. Despite this, in most areas, the two communities live in daily contact with each other. Northern Ireland does not experience the high levels of segregation of many other conflicts such as Israel, South Africa or even some inner cities in North America or Europe. ATQ Stewart summarised it very well when he said that the essence of the Ulster question is not that the two communities cannot live together, but that they do live together and have done for centuries.[2]

The resulting mixture of contact and separation greatly complicates feelings about identity or allegiances. Far from creating conditions where both communities live comfortably among their own people, allegiances in Northern Ireland reflect constant uneasiness. Northern Catholics often aspire to Irish unity, yet sometimes feel alien and are regarded as alien in the south. Northern Protestants almost unanimously want closer union with Britain – hence are unionists – but almost unanimously distrust Britain.

So attitudes remain suspicious, or at least cautious. Nevertheless, since the reforms were implemented, there has been much greater acceptance that they are here to stay, and also that they are fair. The reforms are not only operating, but in themselves have shifted attitudes. The shift has been, not towards a greater tolerance, but towards reluctant acceptance of minority rights. Northern Ireland's experience shows that there is no need to wait until attitudes become more tolerant before introducing reforms. Changes in attitudes can be driven by changes in behaviour, and both can be encouraged by legislative reforms, and institutional changes.

More recent developments, however, indicate that there has been a price to pay for reforms. Certainly the confidence of the Catholic minority has increased. At the same time Protestant confidence has been eroded. Reforms, especially in connection with fair employment, were regarded as advantaging Catholics. The same political changes which have pleased Catholics were viewed by Protestants as the start of a sell-out. The determination of the Orange Order to march past a Catholic area on Portadown's Garvaghy Road in 1995 and 1996 was partly specific to the locality, but also arose from a more general feeling that too many concessions had been made to the minority since the 1960s, what David Trimble described as 'a litany of retreat, surrender and concessions'. The irony is that unionists are increasingly using the same rhetoric that nationalists had been using for decades, about the legitimate expression of cultural identity. The Catholic minority is behaving less like a minority and the Protestant community more like one.

All of these changes have been implemented to a background of sustained violence. Apart from increasing fear, distrust and intransigence, violence imposes another obstacle to reform. A culture of violence has certainly evolved since the 1960s – it would have been surprising if it had not. People's lives have been directly affected by violence. The impact of the Troubles on investment, employment, the tourist industry has been enormous. In a population of around a million and a half, very few do not have a relative or close friend who has suffered from the violence. Almost 3,500 have died; ten times that number were wounded. In some localities the dominant role model has become the paramilitary hero, the hunger striker, the racketeer connected to the paramilitant organisations. The child who has not aspired in those directions is the deviant.

These were active demonstrations of a culture of violence. The culture of violence is also manifested passively. Those who oppose it, even by the act of opposition, are also subject to it. Hence many people react to the culture of violence by seeking either to deny or to escape it. In Northern Ireland, for example, there was a measurable decline in the willingness of people to watch the local television news during the height of the Troubles. I have two sons, aged 29 and 28, young men, who have no memory of the years before the violence. The culture of violence has affected them both, in their case negatively. Both have left Northern Ireland, as have many of their peers, and are now working in Europe and Britain.

In contrast the culture of peace has been weak. The peace movements have flared up only briefly. The strength of opposition to the ending of the IRA ceasefire last year could not be mobilised and petered out in despair. If peace processes may best be understood as the state of tension between a culture of violence and a culture of peace, the culture of violence is vastly more powerful in Northern Ireland. It will take time to change that.

Pluralist choices

So where do we go from here? I believe that every divided society faces three broad options: whether to secede or find a way to work within existing boundaries; whether to aim to resolve conflicts, or settle for regulating them; whether to seek the assimilation of conflicting groups, or to accept and support the differences between them.

Secession or accommodation?

The demand to secede from an existing state is the most radical expression of ethnic difference. It indicates that a dissident group within the state has not confidence that its aspirations can be met within existing boundaries and has determined to create its own state. The attractiveness of this alternative, especially for long-standing colonial or nationalist conflicts, is demonstrated by the post-war rise in member states of the United Nations from 72 to 186. But the experience of secession, most notably in the former Yugoslavia, has not always been successful.

Northern Ireland was the product of a botched attempt at secession. The desire of the majority in Ireland at the start of the 20th century to separate from Britain was frustrated by a concentrated minority in the northern part of the island. The island was partitioned in 1921. Since then, this minority, converted into a majority within Northern Ireland, has itself been frustrated by a substantial minority within the new jurisdiction. Ireland does not provide a convincing exemplar for secession.

Conflict resolution or conflict regulation?

If secession or partition is ruled out, the next dilemma is whether it is ever possible to resolve conflict, or more realistic to recognise that conflict is a social norm rather than an aberration. If the latter view is accepted, perhaps we should plan accordingly to accommodate differences.

To research this compromise a distinction needs to be made between conflict and violence. The use of violence marks the failure of normal means of conflict resolution – political change, negotiation, compromise.

Applying this argument to the conflict in Northern Ireland, it suggests that all the ideologically determined 'solutions' – a united Ireland, integration with Britain, an independent Northern Ireland – aspire towards an unrealisable permanence. None of these could guarantee stability. A united Ireland carries the risk of creating a substantial Protestant minority, concentrated in one part of the island and entrenched against the new arrangements. Integration with

Britain is unacceptable to everyone, including the British, except a minority within the unionist community. An independent Ulster is the least feasible option of all, for political and economic reasons. This leaves as the only serious option a compromise arrangement which seeks to satisfy through negotiations the aspirations of all interests in Northern Ireland. It would need to carry a battery of strong and enforceable guarantees for all parties including protection of minority rights, a charter on human rights, rewards for political co-operation, sanctions against majoritarianism and frequent monitoring. And it would need an external review body with sufficient weight to monitor developments and enforce fair treatment for all.

Assimilation or pluralism?

This brings us to the third dilemma. If conflict resolution is ruled out in favour of conflict regulation, what broad strategy options are available to deal with it, and what light does the Northern Ireland experience throw on them? If one assumes that certain policy approaches to plural societies – genocide, apartheid, the suppression of human rights – are morally unacceptable, governments faced with ethnic minorities have two broad strategic approaches available to them: policies of assimilation or policies of pluralism.

Policies of assimilation emphasise the integrity of the national unit and approach minority issues as individual rather than group problems. The background philosophy is that, if all are treated equally before the law and fairly in other respects, there is less need to recognise and protect the rights of particular groups. Underlying this approach for many of its advocates is the hope that fair government will diminish group differences in time, leading eventually to assimilation of different ethnic groups into a corporate citizenship. If cultural diversity is not fully respected, however, assimilation may amount to the establishment of a dominant culture, to which other groups are expected to conform. Examples of countries which adopt broadly assimilative approaches, at least until recently, are France and the United States.

Policies of pluralism emphasise the need to accept that some ethnic differences are unlikely to disappear and that separate groups should be given both parity of esteem and substantial control over their own affairs. In their most extreme form, pluralist approaches may recognise that ethnic and other differences between groups are sufficiently strong to justify dividing the states into smaller states, as has happened between Belgium and Holland, in the Indian sub-continent and, more recently, in the former Czechoslovakia and the former Yugoslavia. A less dramatic approach is to establish a decentralised federal state with relatively weak central structures, and with considerable powers devolved to the regions. Regional devolution has operated successfully in Switzerland for centuries, and is currently being implemented in the Basque region of Spain. It is more difficult in countries where ethnic groups do not live in geographically separate districts, but even there a form of what might be described as administrative devolution may be possible. This incorporates structures based on ethnic, religious or other differences into the system of government, and devolves to each ethnic group considerable control over its own resources.

Northern Ireland can show examples of both assimilative and pluralist policies operating in parallel. During the 1970s government policies were predominantly assimilative. The introduction of electoral reforms, the Fair Employment Act 1976 and the move to a centralised administration of housing set out to protect individual rights before the law. There were also pluralist structures functioning alongside them: almost all children attended predominantly Catholic or Protestant schools; certain sports were almost exclusively played by one or other community; organisations like the Orange Order, the Apprentice Boys of Derry and the Ancient Order of Hibernians catered exclusively for one tradition; the Irish language, music and folklore was largely, but not exclusively, the province of Catholics. The recent encouragement of cultural diversity in the establishment of integrated and Irish-language schools alongside the existing segregated systems, and increased encouragement of cultural diversity, represent a further shift toward pluralism.

This mixed approach may be subject to attack for lack of purity. It is the only realistic short-term one. Perhaps I should come out of the closet at this point and confess that I am a gut assimilationist – but not an unrealistic one. It seems to me that suspicion between the two communities in Northern Ireland will continue while the central constitutional conundrum remains unresolved. So, to put it in the most begrudging terms possible, I believe there is presently no alternative to the move towards pluralism, but towards a pluralism aware of its own limitations and dangers. Pluralist approaches are not a panacea for divided societies. Indeed they can be positively dangerous unless accompanied by clear and effective legal procedures, and by an unacceptable means of arbitrating between competing rights. The flying of the Union Jack in the workplace, for example, may be presented as an expression of their culture by unionist workers, but seen by nationalists as intimidatory or provocative. I am concerned too that, for some extremists, the ultimate expression of one's culture is to remove those who do not share it, by intimidation or even murder. Despite these reservations, I am attracted by the idea of encouraging cultural diversity as a stage towards a society more relaxed about its differences.

The Dutch experience provides an interesting example of the advantages and the dangers of such an approach. At the start of the century Holland tried to tackle its internal differences, which at that time were mainly religious – by giving the different sectors in society – Protestant, Catholic and secular – substantial control over their own resources. Each sector was allowed, in fact encouraged, to institutionalise these divisions and to develop its own schools, universities, trade unions, hospitals, political parties and later radio and television stations. The philosophy was that distrust of the system and of each other was the root of the problem. If agreement could be reached between the sectors about fair allocation of resources, these would be distributed within the sectors, and you had the basis of a functioning system. This system operated in Holland for 50 years. In Dutch it was known as *verzuiling*.

Dutch inspiration is also responsible for another, better known, system for dealing with social divisions through deliberate separation, in one of its further colonies. The system operated in South Africa for 30 years. In Dutch the system was known as *apartheid*.

The lesson is clear: that there are dangers implicit in making separations between different segments in society, and delicacy is required in order to make the system work. The difference between *verzuiling* and *apartheid* lies in the systematic process which implemented them. In the first, all major segments were partners in the government. In the second, the majority of citizens were excluded from a system whose function was the control of one group by another. It is naïve to pretend that there is not a danger of seepage from one to the other.

NOTES

1. George E. Simpson and J. Milton Yinger, *Racial and Cultural Minorities* (Harper & Row, 1965).
2. See A.T.Q. Stewart, *The Narrow Ground* (Faber, 1977).

CULTURAL ROUTES: WAYS OF APPROACHING DIVERSITY

Jonathan Bardon

Sitting here in calm, academic surroundings well calculated to promote dispassionate reflection, in the heart of the leafy and tranquil
suburbs of South Belfast, it does not immediately spring to mind that
we are meeting in a provincial capital plagued by political and sectarian violence since 1969. A quarter-century and more of conflict
gives Northern Ireland the unenviable record of being the most con-
tinuously disturbed region in Europe since the end of the Second
World War and, possibly, since the beginning of the century. Well over
3,000 people have met with violent deaths during the 'the Troubles'
– our euphemism for the blood-letting and destruction. It is not a full-
scale civil war, however: last July, while Northern Ireland was convulsed by the confrontation at Drumcree, bodies were being
unearthed in Bosnia, providing grim evidence that the slaughter of
just a few days in 1995 at Srebrenica and Bukovar equalled the death
toll from intercommunal and political conflict since 1969 in Ulster.
Nevertheless, in a population of barely 1.6 million the violence has
touched almost every family in the region.

I would have no difficulty spending the rest of this talk – indeed the
remainder of the day – attempting to explain why Northern Ireland
is so chronically troubled. For the benefit of those who have come
from beyond our shores let me try to summarise. The origins of the
deep divisions go back to the devastating subjugation of the Gaelic
north at the end of the 16th century and the subsequent 17th-century
colonisation by Protestant British settlers. Outnumbered and sur-
rounded in most districts, the incomers lived in constant fear of being
attacked and dispossessed by fiercely resentful natives who differed
sharply from them in religion, language and cultural traditions. And
this occurred when much of Europe was being convulsed by intense
religious conflict and so in Ulster, the northern province of Ireland,
sectarian antagonism became a critical ingredient in the maturing
lethal brew.

Wounds were not given time to heal. There were massacres perpe-
trated by both sides and further confiscations of land. When in 1689
James II chose Ireland as his springboard for attempting to recover
the English throne with the help of a French army, the island briefly
and for the only time in its history became the cockpit of Europe. The
defeat of the forces of the Catholic King James (at Derry in 1689, the
Boyne in 1690, and Aughrim in 1691) ensured the survival of the
northern Protestant colony – these triumphs are still celebrated by
Ulster loyalists from year to year. There were 3,160 parades in 1996:
2,404 of them are classified by the Royal Ulster Constabulary as 'loyalist' and the vast majority celebrate those 17th-century victories.

Even a century of peace thereafter could not erase the fear and
resentment deeply etched in the folk memory. In the late 18th century a fierce sectarian warfare erupted in the densely-populated
counties of south-central Ulster, one outcome being the formation of
the Orange Order in 1795. In the 19th century tens of thousands of
people from impoverished rural Ulster poured into Belfast, enjoying
remarkable industrial and commercial success. There, in the narrow
streets of the fastest-growing urban centre in the United Kingdom,
immigrants from mid-Ulster re-enacted the sectarian conflicts of
their forbears. By then ancient hatreds were being inflamed by uncertainty about Ireland's constitutional future.

When Northern Ireland came into being in 1921 its devolved government did little to assuage sectarian rivalries but it did not create
them, it inherited them. The outbreak of violence in 1969 had complex political causes and the present instability of Northern Ireland is
political, yet the main reason why the Troubles have persisted is that
they are fuelled by cataclysmic events long ago. In short, in contemporary Europe, Northern Ireland is a region with its share and more
of cultural diversity.

Until the end of the 1980s there was a widespread tendency to
regard the Northern Ireland 'problem' as being a curious and unique
historical survival. The disintegration of the Soviet bloc at the other
end of Europe indicated otherwise. A decade ago very few would have
predicted the direction and the extraordinary rate of change there
following the revolution in Romania and the dismantling of the
Berlin Wall. We in the West rejoiced to see millions enjoying a new-
found freedom which cleared the way for an open society and representative democracy.

At the same time the collapse of the previous centralised power
structures allowed long-dormant ethnic rivalries to gush to the sur-

face. As Armenians and Azeris, and Serbs, Croats and Muslims, and Moldovans and Transdniestrians slaughtered each other it was plain that they were impelled by atavistic urges remarkably parallel to those fuelling the Troubles in Northern Ireland. Let me read you this extract from a newspaper report for 7 December 1991:

> In green fields men mutter darkly of vendetta, unconsciously plunging between the centuries in mid-sentence. Mortal enemies stalk each other from a distance of five miles. Hatred burns so bright that vengeful young killers smirk and boast of their murders to strangers. It is an enclosed world of bowel-shaking fear, cold joyous revenge, dark paranoia and venomous suspicion. And the fields are watered with the blood of men.

That could have been written about Nagorno-Karabakh, or from Mostar or Sarajevo or anywhere in Bosnia-Herzegovina, or indeed from Rwanda: in fact it is a report by Kevin Toolis on County Tyrone in the *Guardian*. What is reported is one manifestation of cultural diversity which cannot be ignored. It is, of course, also a political problem in need of a political solution. Such a solution has proved elusive, not because there isn't one but because the intercommunal division is so deep. In the meantime the cultural diversity is there and no political formula, no matter how ingenious, is going to spirit it away.

Let me now be more specific about the approaches adopted in Northern Ireland; I shall go back to 1981 when, after an apparent gradual reduction in the intensity of violence in the late 1970s, the conflict acquired a new intensity: republican prisoners went on hunger strike and ten of them starved themselves to death. Never had society here seemed so bitterly divided and never did the political future look bleaker. There has always been a tendency for the intelligentsia of Ulster to say 'a plague on both your houses' and – apart from painting pictures, writing plays, poems and novels, and composing symphonies – detach themselves from public life. In the early 1980s a number of academics, writers and artists felt that attitudes would have to change. For example a great deal of careful, painstaking research which explained the conflict and challenged assumptions on both sides was remaining locked up in academic journals, written in esoteric styles quite baffling to the general public. One of the first initiatives was the formation of the Two Traditions Group, chaired by Canon Eric Elliott. Members of this quickly discovered that even the professionals were often ignorant of relevant work in other disciplines. Eventually the work of the Group attracted the attention of senior civil servants, themselves frantically searching for ways out of the impasse.

In 1986 Mari Fitzduff and Hugh Frazer delivered their report, 'Improving Community Relations' to the Standing Advisory Commission on Human Rights. It recommended that the Secretary of State for Northern Ireland create a new unit to promote better community relations and reduce religious discrimination. The result was the formation in 1987 of the Central Community Relations Unit. Two senior civil servants drafted into the unit listened attentively to calls for a cultural heritage initiative, from the Two Traditions Group in particular. The outcome was the setting up of the Cultural Traditions Group (CTG) in 1988; Dr James Hawthorne, just stepping down as Controller of BBC Northern Ireland became the first chairman. As Dr Hawthorne recalled himself:

> Our first conversations veered between hope and cynicism but the discussions moved really well. Before long there was not only great accord but a new-found enthusiasm to solve problems which individually we had been grappling with for years.

Meanwhile a hurricane of change was blowing through the Northern Ireland Department of Education. The force 11 was Dr Brian Mawhinney, an Ulsterman who as MP for Peterborough had been appointed the region's Education Minister. He pushed through legislation to provide recognition and funding for integrated schools where the children of Catholics, Protestants, other religions and no religion could be educated together There are now 30 integrated schools serving around 2 per cent of Northern Ireland's school population. Funding for joint work between pupils attending Catholic and Protestant schools was increased. A new curriculum for all pupils of compulsory school attendance age produced dramatic change in the classroom. The special feature distinguishing the Northern Ireland Curriculum from that elsewhere in the United Kingdom were the cross-curricular themes: I chaired the working groups which made recommendations on two of these, Cultural Heritage, and Education for Mutual Understanding. You will hear more about these later in the conference but, in short, pupils for the first time were required to look at each others' traditions and culture. For example, until then a great many Protestant schools avoided studying any Irish history and many Catholic schools avoided British history. Very few bothered with local history and a survey by Jack Magee made the surprising revelation that quite a few Catholic schools did no Irish history because there were not enough questions on it in public examinations. Now all pupils have to study local history, and aspects of Irish history, British history, European history and world history.

This change in the schools was to keep the new Cultural Traditions Group very busy. In 1990 Dr Mawhinney set up the Northern Ireland Community Relations Council (CRC) as a publicly-funded, grant-giving limited company with charitable status and he decided that the Cultural Traditions Group should be united with it, continuing as a sub-committee. Up to this the CTG had been advising government departments on how best to advance cross-community contact and now, more and more, it took on this role itself. A series of major conferences extended the discussion to a wider influential group, especially decision-makers in such fields as education, community theatre, museums, the arts agencies, publishing and the media. The first conference, 'Varieties of Irishness' (at which Dr Roy Foster gave the keynote address) was held in Portrush in March 1989. The following year came 'Varieties of Britishness' and in 1991 'All Europeans Now?' Thereafter conferences were smaller and tackled more specific issues. The Group was refining its aims and objectives. Dr Hawthorne gave the flavour of this in an interview with a journalist:

> It recognises the value and legitimacy of tradition and seeks to celebrate cultural diversity in a non-threatening way . . . There is no search for an elusive common culture and no theory that one actually exists. There are many colours in our cultural spectrum, not just green and orange. Mixing them would only produce an unattractive shade of brown.

Paul Sweeney, an influential founder member of the CRC, reinforces Dr Hawthorne's last point:

> I think it's too narrow to say there are two communities in Northern Ireland. My own experience is that there are literally hundreds, maybe thousands of communities, all with their own definition of their own community and their own sense of place.

In a lecture at Queen's University in November 1990 Dr Maurice Hayes, second Chairman of the CTG, warned:

But to see the two main cultural groupings as monoliths is to erect stereotypes and much of the difficulty in understanding Northern Ireland is not only in the creation of stereotypes by and for outsiders, but the fact that we create our own stereotypes, and then begin to live up to them and believe in them ourselves.

The CRC is publicly-funded and the awarding of grants is an important part of its work. An early shortcoming identified was the lack of publications which could be used to stimulate greater and wider appreciation and understanding of Northern Ireland's diverse cultural heritage. There were teachers out there, often middle-aged and older, who had never taught local history or Irish history and were now required to do so. They desperately needed texts, for example. Northern Ireland has a limited, specialised market unattractive to national publishers who need to sell at least 10,000 copies of a book for viability. A Publications Committee of the CRC provides grants to local publishers where appropriate: by lowering the price of each book the readership is increased and much good work is printed which might never have seen the light of day. In the words of Maurna Crozier, who has worked with the CTG from the outset: 'The hope is that the Cultural Traditions Publications Scheme will have a legacy of texts which help people in Northern Ireland during and after a significant period in their history'. The Blackstaff Press, one of the local publishers assisted, was chosen as the Sunday Times Small Publisher of the Year in 1992. Anne Tannahill, the Managing Director, writes:

When the sense of identity is as circumscribed and confused as it is in the north of Ireland, the rediscovery of our own ancestral voices and the thoughtful articulation of our present predicament became crucial . . . As well as helping to explain ourselves to ourselves within our respective communities and in the process cultivating proper self-esteem as well as much needed self-criticism, we hope that the 500 plus titles published by Blackstaff have helped each community to understand the other one better. Ignorance is the common starting-point in the ghastly downward spiral that moves through fear to hatred to murder to more fear, more hatred, *ad nauseam.*

Another busy committee is that dealing with Local Cultural Traditions. A key aspect of this programme is debate, in a manner which offers opportunities for people to talk in safe, neutral and friendly surroundings. The Committee supports groups organising conferences, seminars and workshops which address the questions of identity, allegiance, division, diversity, pluralism and the like. Groups which set up projects specifically aimed at ensuring wide participation get much of the funding. Examples include: community drama groups; women's, writers' and musical groups; and local history and heritage organisations. The Committee is particularly concerned to encourage local community groups to engage new audiences in debate on issues of identity and belonging. The CTG can only be concerned with those above the compulsory school leaving age of 16; those who fall below that age are the responsibility of the Department of Education. The CTG has long been concerned to reach those aged between 16 and 25 – partly because they are the most vulnerable to subversion by paramilitary organisations but mainly because they represent the future. This helps to explain why the committee extends support to struggling drama groups and musical events.

The Media Committee gives far fewer grants than LCT but in larger lumps. The skill to be acquired here was to avoid funding anything that could be considered propaganda. Ways were found to encourage BBC Northern Ireland and Ulster Television to increase the scale and scope of local documentary and community-based programmes, and to get independent programme-makers to tender, to invite them to submit ideas 'which in the opinion of the Group, can contribute to a better understanding of cultural diversity and community within Northern Ireland'. Those accepted included 'Plain Tales from Northern Ireland', a six-part documentary series broadcast throughout the UK on BBC2 in 1993: based on Carlo Gébler's book *The Glass Curtain*, which focused on the lives and attitudes of people living in the border county of Fermanagh.

Other work by the CTG includes support for the Irish language which led on directly to the formation of the Ultach Trust with government financial support in September 1989; financial help for the Ulster Scots Language Society, its magazine *Ullans* and books on weaver poets; the launching of *Causeway*, a journal of cultural traditions, in 1993; Cultural Heritage Resources fairs of benefit to teachers, school groups, youth workers, library staff and local history activists; the giving of awards; and cultural traditions fellowships, on topics such as symbols, music or dialects; the appointment of county workers to give talks on the work of the cultural traditions programme; and the organisation of exhibitions such as the most recent on 'Popular Belief' in co-operation with the Arts Council and Clotworthy Arts Centre. This is a touring exhibition like the most ambitious one, the 'Symbols' exhibition, opened at Belfast City Hall in October 1994 and taken to Strasbourg and Frankfurt.

It was while we were in Strasbourg with the Symbols exhibition in October 1996 that Sean Nolan obtained a copy of 'In From the Margins', a report prepared for the Council of Europe by the European Task Force on Culture and Development. We found the views expressed there dovetailed remarkably with our own thinking over the past nine years. If you get the opportunity to consult it, turn to paragraph 3.4 entitled 'The keys to cultural policy'.

In constantly contemplating our own navel in Northern Ireland we sometimes forget that others in the same continent also have long experience of celebrating, enduring or otherwise managing cultural diversity. At the beginning of this century most Europeans were citizens not of nation states but of multinational empires – the Austro-Hungarian, Russian, Turkish, German and British. In the Austro-Hungarian Empire, for example, the nations included Germans, Magyars, Italians, Poles, Czechs, Slovaks, Ruthenes, Little Russians, White Russians, Romanians, Serbs, Croats, Muslims, Slovenes, Jews and Gypsies. In seeking national self-determination the Czechs demanded the lands of the Crown of King Wenceslas (the one who looked out, the first Christian ruler of Bohemia) and Magyars insisted on the lands of the Crown of King Stephen (the first Christian ruler of Hungary): both claims included Slovakia, given no say in the contest. If all these peoples asked for nation states at once, then there would be no Austro-Hungarian Empire left.

There were so many nationalities in the Austrian Empire, all with overlapping and clashing aspirations, that the Czech patriot Palacký concluded in despair that if the Habsburg Empire did not exist it would be necessary to create it. The imperial rulers had their own ways of dealing with contemporary cultural diversity: the German Kaiser pretended the Polish, Danish and French minorities did not exist; Tsar Nicholas enthusiastically launched pogroms against Jews and other upstart nationalities demanding self-determination such as the trans-Baikal Buryats; the Sultan sent in Bashi Bazouks to perpetrate Bulgarian horrors; and the British Prime Minister, Lord Salisbury, when asked why he did not support Home Rule for Ireland, remarked: 'You would not confide free representative institutions to the Hottentots, for example'. Actually the Austrians, by the standards of the day, were much more sophisticated and subtle than the other empires – if they over-indulged the Hungarians it did at least stop Serbs, Croats and Slovenes from falling out with each other. Had 'Gaga', that is Franz Josef, not been so foolish as to take the advice of his commander-in-chief, Conrad von Hotzendorff, the Habsburg ethnic stew might have been kept simmering gently without boiling over for another half century.

The Great War changed everything: the only empire of those I mentioned to survive was the British Empire. From the wreckage of these collapsed empires emerged a whole new batch of nation states. It proved impossible, in spite of US President Woodrow Wilson's Fourteen Points, to create single-identity nation states. Of these states only Austria had a fairly homogeneous ethnic composition and it has been estimated that more than 25 million found themselves as national minorities after 1919. Only two-thirds of the inhabitants of Poland spoke Polish, for example, and there were 4.6 million Germans, Poles, Ruthenes and Hungarians in Czechoslovakia out of a total population of 14.3 million. In short, whether they liked it or not (and most of them did not) the governments of these successor states found they had to deal with cultural diversity within their frontiers. Refusal to put in place strategies for recognising and celebrating diversity, together with racist triumphalism and paranoia, led of course to the murder of millions in the 1940s. Careful thinking about cultural diversity in contemporary Europe is in part because there are so many vivid memories of the horrors of that time, not to speak of ethnic cleansing and new brutalities in the early 1990s.

Successes attract less publicity than does violent conflict. Since the Second World War several states have shown that they can contain or reduce ethnic tension by fresh constitutional arrangements. Examples include: autonomy for South Tyrol in 1972; devolved governments in Catalonia and the Basque country after Franco's death in 1975; the creation of the canton of Jura in Switzerland in 1978; a measure of self-government for Corsica in 1982; the evolution of Belgium into a federal state by 1988; and the granting of special status to Transdniestria within Moldova in 1992. In other words, more and more European states are realising that giving due recognition to the cultural diversity within their jurisdictions can not only enrich the lives of all citizens but can also enhance stability. Let me read you an extract from the Council of Europe's 'In From the Margins'.

3.4.7. Europe's diversity is a fact of life, although not one which has always been welcomed by the rulers of nation states and empires.

However, the past 50 years have seen a contrary consensus emerge, most democratic politicians now argue that the protection, even the promotion, of diversity, both in terms of different ways of life as well as of artistic expression, achieves two significant and desirable objectives. The first of these is a recognition of the right to be different . . . [there follows a warning that cultures should not be exempt from critical examination for instance in the cases of Nazi Germany or the Balkan wars].

3.4.8. The second objective concerns the relevance of cultural diversity to development. The notion is that the imposition of a single cultural model would be a break on European development rather than a spur . . .

Let me finish with a recollection. Some years ago I was fishing in a small flat-bottomed boat on Lough Melvin, a lake some five miles long in the north-west. A wild storm blew in from the Atlantic and, as I sculled frantically, I was being driven towards an island. Here cultures had clashed and blended: this was a crannóg, an artificial island constructed in early Christian times on which was the ruined bastion of the McClancys, successfully defended against Sir William Fitzwilliam's troops by Francisco de Cuellar and other Armada castaways in 1588. As I baled my boat in the lee of the island, I looked behind and saw a line of buoys across the eastern end of the lough, making the frontier between Northern Ireland and the Irish Republic.

There is another sort of division in Lough Melvin. The lake is home, not only to perch and salmon, but also to four distinct species of trout: sonaghan, ferox, gillaroo and brown trout which do not interbreed even though they spawn in the same rivers. In short those four varieties of trout in one Irish lough are more genetically distinct than any of the races of human beings to be found anywhere on Earth.

It is all too easy to exaggerate our differences.

APPROACHES TO CULTURAL DIVERSITY IN EUROPE: EDUCATION TOWARDS TOLERANCE

Peter Leuprecht

It is customary at a conference such as this to thank the organisers and congratulate them on their initiative. Given the theme and venue of this conference, my thanks and congratulations take on a special significance. As Jonathan Bardon, Chairman of the Northern Ireland Community Relations Council, wrote in his pre-conference message, the troubles in Northern Ireland constitute the longest-running conflict in Europe since the Second World War. In these circumstances the very organisation of this conference – considering the objectives assigned to it – is an act of courage and commitment.

Cultural diversity today is at the same time a fact of life and a central political issue throughout Europe – and by that I mean the Europe of the Council of Europe with its 40 member states stretching from Connemara to the Caucasus. Before outlining the approach developed and implemented by the Council of Europe in this field, I feel it is important to reiterate a number of fundamental ideas to which I attach a great deal of importance. The first is that cultural diversity is nothing new or exceptional. On the contrary, it is clear from the whole history of our continent that the multiplicity and cohabitation of different cultures in the same geographical area is a constant feature of the cultural reality of Europe. The extent of this abundance and variety of identities and cultures is quite remarkable. In a study on the ethnic origins of Europeans, the historian and linguist François Georges Cerbelaud Salagnac identified over 250 peoples who had settled in Europe at various points in history. These peoples, themselves from a variety of origins, have met each other, sometimes violently, sometimes more peacefully, thereby creating innumerable yet distinctive intercultural patterns. It is therefore futile to seek in today's Europe a culture which is not the result of cross-breeding. In other words, I am convinced that every European culture is the product of cultural diversity.

The second idea I would like to stress is that cultural diversity is not a threat to each individual culture but rather the very essence of its survival and creativity. Cultures are not static; indeed any culture or identity which does not grow and develop is doomed to atrophy. But a culture which can accommodate difference and open up to the world is a living culture, capable of creating new impulses and new meanings. The major stages in the cultural history of Europe, in other words those periods when it was a source of new ideas and opened up to new philosophies of life and human destiny, have been characterised by an ability to accept otherness, be this from within the continent, from the periphery or from other places further afield. It is this multiethnic and multicultural environment that has produced the most enriching contributions to European literature, science, philosophy and art. It is worth remembering that each of these fertile periods was the result of a victory of openness and tolerance over obscurantism.

And as a last introductory remark, I would like to stress that cultural diversity is not only a social or community phenomenon. It is also an individual reality which all of us experience in our own personal and family history. Each and every one of us belongs to national, regional, local, religious, linguistic or professional cultures which make up our cultural individuality, and the uniqueness and richness of our personality. In this sense, as the anthropologist Claude Lévi-Strauss repeatedly points out, coming into contact with other cultures is always an act of discovering or rediscovering oneself. 'The discovery of togetherness', he wrote, 'is the discovery of a relationship, not a barrier.' If, as I believe, cultural diversity is the norm and a precondition for cultural dynamism and innovation, why then is there a problem today?

Since the beginning of the 1990s, Europe has experienced a major upheaval and the vision it formed of itself during the 40 years of the Cold War has been turned upside down. This vision was one of a bipolar Europe where everything was cut and dried and the rules clearly defined, even though the situation in itself was intolerable, particularly for the peoples of central and eastern Europe. The division of Europe was profoundly anti-historical and anti-cultural. The fall of the Iron Curtain and the possibility for the former communist countries to take the path to democracy clearly give cause for celebration and hope. On the cultural level, the end of this ideological bipolarity and the opening of the borders provided an opportunity to rediscover an even richer diversity of European culture. But we also know that this European revolution has created a series of potentially dangerous and extremely worrying side-effects; the breakdown of economic structures, the resurgence of aggressive nationalism, xenophobia, anti-semitism and the rejection of minorities. Moreover, such problems as racism and ethnic or religious intolerance are endemic in the older democracies of western Europe too, as I hardly need to remind you here in Northern Ireland.

The question currently facing us is not one of accepting or rejecting cultural diversity, but of how, in the new geopolitical context, it should be handled to ensure it has the best possible chance of leading to peace, creativity and a brighter future. The question is not whether we are going to live together in our heterogeneity and diversity, but how are we going to frame this living together. Before replying to this question, I should perhaps put the idea of cultural diversity in Europe into perspective. Over and beyond cultural differences, there are a number of shared basic values: respect for the equal dignity of every human being – the very foundation of human rights; the search for the best possible form of political organisation; pluralist democracy; and the rule of law.

Set up in 1949 in the wake of the Second World War, the Council of Europe was given a double mandate: first, as the instrument of co-operation between European states in addressing their common problems with a view to achieving greater unity; and second, as guarantor of the values trampled underfoot during the war and, more specifically, during the Holocaust and associated acts of genocide. 'Never again' was the motto of the founding fathers. Whereas today European co-operation and integration are often presented as being first and foremost an economic matter, I would like to remind you that the original objective of European integration was peace and the defence of fundamental values. At the first Council of Europe Summit of Heads of State and Government, held in Vienna in 1993, the latter solemnly stated in their Declaration:

> The end of the division of Europe offers an historic opportunity to consolidate peace and stability on the continent. All our countries are committed to pluralist and parliamentary democracy, the indivisibility and universality of human rights, the rule of law and a common cultural heritage enriched by its diversity. Europe can thus become a vast area of democratic security.
>
> This Europe is a source of immense hope which must in no event be destroyed by territorial ambitions, the resurgence of aggressive

nationalism, the perpetuation of spheres of influence, intolerance
or totalitarian ideologists.

In fact, the Council of Europe has striven to promote, develop and
defend these values since its inception.

On the legal and political level, a number of fundamental texts
were adopted, the first being the European Convention on Human
Rights and the most recent relating to the protection of minorities
and their languages. In this way we have built up a body of doctrine,
basic documents and practices which constitutes a safeguard against
abuse, but which is also constantly evolving.

The founding fathers were fully aware, however, that action in the
legal field and the drafting of conventions alone were not enough.
Without an active strategy for winning the hearts and minds of men
and women, the effort would be in vain. Among the various instru-
ments to hand, education is surely one of the most important. That is
why co-operation in the field of education and culture has featured
in the Council's programme from the outset. This too was reasserted
in the Vienna Declaration. The Heads of State and Government
expressed their conviction that

> cultural co-operation, for which the Council of Europe is a prime
> instrument – through education, the media, cultural action, the
> protection and the enhancement of the cultural heritage and par-
> ticipation of young people – is essential for creating a cohesive yet
> diverse Europe.

Whether we like it or not – and personally I do like it – in the Europe
of today we are living in a multicultural society. This multicultural
nature of European society is here to stay. The Council of Europe
therefore strongly argues the case for intercultural education. In our
changing world, education cannot confine itself to reproducing and
transmitting a cultural heritage – and certainly not a single cultural
heritage; it necessarily performs other functions. I agree with Alain
Tourain when he writes:

> A definite stand must . . . be taken against the identification of edu-
> cation with a particular community and, consequently, a given cul-
> ture and society . . . he democratic spirit, of which pluralism is a
> fundamental component, cannot be confined to the political
> arena; it must be applied likewise to culture as a whole.

Indeed, we must strive not only for political, but also for cultural pluralism. We must learn to regard dissimilarity and diversity not as an encumbrance, but as what it really is: a tremendous enrichment.

In this spirit, the Council of Europe has in recent years stepped up its action in the field of education, and the Committee of Ministers in a Resolution adopted in December 1995 laid down the following objectives:

◌ fostering democratic values and human rights according to a common cultural approach;
◌ building confidence and mutual respect between nations and communities;
◌ promoting awareness of the cultural community of the new Europe enriched by its diversity.

The main objective of this action is to build an open and tolerant democratic society. It is to help young people:

◌ to learn how to apprehend, understand and accept other cultures;
◌ to develop their judgement on the basis of open-mindedness, reliable information and in a spirit of seeking the truth;
◌ to avoid stereotypes, over-simplifications and manipulations.

All this was given practical expression in the organisation of a major European campaign against racism, anti-semitism, xenophobia and intolerance which made millions of young people aware of the questions which concern us today. Unfortunately, in spite of all the efforts to combat intolerance in all its forms, this scourge persists, and this country has in recent days experienced shocking manifestations of it. I am referring to the burning of churches.

In the field of education, we in the Council of Europe have concentrated our effort on promoting the same goals in specific fields which are of direct relevance to us here at this conference. A first project, entitled 'Democracy, Human Rights, Minorities, Educational and Cultural Aspects' was rounded off with a final conference in the summer of 1997. It has helped identify not only the guiding principles but also the ways and means of ensuring positive management of cultural diversity in a democratic society. This year has seen the launching of a new project on education for democratic citizenship. Its aim is to show first of all how, on the threshold of the 21st century, it is possible to define a concept of democratic and European citizenship which, without challenging loyalty to a freely-chosen national identity and culture, will lead to new forms of solidarity and acknowledgement of diversity as a contributing factor in achieving stronger unity. The Council of Europe has done, and is doing, very substantial work in the field of human rights education, which we also see as a means of imparting respect for, and solidarity with, others, and as an education for the peaceful settlement of conflicts. We are also continuing to pay special attention to history teaching, with a new project intended to promote the teaching of 20th-century European history in secondary schools.

Following the collapse of communism, the history books have had to be re-written in the countries of central and eastern Europe, and the teachers have had to learn to lay aside the ideological straitjacket in which they previously had to lead their professional lives. But at the same time some newly independent states are tending to use history teaching as a means of promoting national consciousness. They are certainly not the first to do so. But it does raise the question as to how far such use of history teaching is legitimate and what its consequences are. In western Europe, people have had much more time to get used to openly multicultural situations and to the whole concept of European unity. Yet every day we see evidence that we are still a long way from general positive acceptance of this evolution. That is why we need to reconsider the question of nationalist attitudes which are assimilated in early years and reinforced, maybe unconsciously, by the school system.

Not only here in Northern Ireland but in every conflict between national, ethnic or religious communities, historical events are invoked to justify contemporary attitudes and actions. The mythology of one's own community, through being called history – and there is usually an element of historical truth in it – comes to be regarded as indisputable and is taken to justify acts which are committed in its name.

In the face of this kind of challenge education cannot, of course, achieve rapid results. It always works for the longer term. But somehow we have to lay the basis to ensure that the coming generation is less receptive to the rhetoric of exclusion and hatred.

I see that educational basis as lying in the development of the capacity for critical judgement and dialogue, in an appreciation of the other's point of view, in the explanation of how historical events or cultural realities – but not universal human rights or basic democratic values – can be perceived in different ways. This is maybe the most important task of the Council of Europe in this field. We must insist that other countries, other peoples, other communities should not be (as they unfortunately so often are) treated anonymously and collectively (the Serbs, the Croats, the Germans, the Catholics, the Protestants), but shown in their diversity. When we learn of our own people's achievements, mention should also be made of those of our neighbours. In our history teaching we must find room not only for the injustice we have suffered at the hands of others, but also for the injustice we may have inflicted upon others and for the contribution of those others to our own culture.

The Council of Europe has done much to encourage the development of programmes which seek to remove prejudice by emphasising positive mutual influences between different countries, religions and ideas in the historical development of Europe. It has accumulated a good deal of experience in combating intolerance and promoting mutual understanding, not least thanks to its networks of decision-makers and experts. But we need a constant renewal and enrichment of our outlook and approach from the practical experience of those who are working on the ground. In the last resort it may be the grass-roots initiatives, often modest but undertaken with courage and persistence, that really count.

The approach we have adopted in the implementation of the various activities I have mentioned is very close to that opted for by organisers of this Conference, and I find this very gratifying. We have to combine fundamental reflection, action in the field, dissemination of good practices and above all the creation of networks of willing and well-intentioned men and women who can learn to understand each other, compare their problems and share their practical experiences. Northern Ireland has a very rich experience in this field, as I had the opportunity to appreciate on the occasion of my visit a year ago.

In this way we can hope – and I firmly believe this hope is not misplaced – that little by little, Europe and Europeans will learn how to cope, peacefully, with all the various challenges of the renewed cultural diversity of our continent. They will be able to enter the third millennium not taking a step backwards to the ideas of the 19th century, but with new approaches which augur well for the future. I am convinced that this conference will help to point the way down that road.

DOES TELEVISION MATTER?

Paddy Coulter

The previous speakers have established that in contemporary
Europe, diversity is a fact of life. So right across Europe we have this
move towards acceptance of a multicultural, multinational society.
This gives a real headache to broadcasters, and particularly to
national broadcasters.

I would like to say at the outset that broadcasters do not usually set
out to create racism and xenophobia. There are exceptions, and I will
come back to that. What broadcasters have is a choice – quite a stark
choice. The choice is between ignoring this trend in our society –
what I would term the 'business as usual' option – or making cultural
pluralism part of television reality.

I would first like to make out a basic case for broadcasting. Does
television reality really matter? There is a school of thought – very
fashionable in postmodernist Britain – that television is superficial
and ephemeral and that its impact is hard to measure. These accusations are difficult to counter and there is quite an industry in Britain
today trying to support them. A survey by the reputable Leicester
University Department of Mass Communications goes as far as to say
that when television sets are turned on in this country they are not
necessarily being watched. The survey showed people doing a whole
range of activities in front of their sets, making meals, for example, or
even making love, and nothing in the survey suggested that the programmes were having the impact that their makers thought they
were. So the dominant view is that television does not matter, or is
merely entertainment. This is a very sophisticated view. However, it is
a view which I would challenge head-on. My view is that television
matters enormously. I have no academic research to back me up on
this – but I hardly need it when advertisers spend millions of pounds
trying to get their message across on television. During an election
campaign, for example, spin doctors use this mass-medium to try to
get their message across.

If we look at other countries we see that it is of enormous importance who owns and controls the national broadcasters. In many countries it is the government which does so, and this is disturbing. Surveys here and abroad show that, overwhelmingly, people get their information about the world from television (and from radio as well, but I shall confine myself to talking about television as it is my particular area of competence). So for the public of Europe, for example, one poll showed that 84 per cent of people get this kind of information from television. Survey after survey shows a similar huge majority.

I now want to point out some trends in broadcasting which are affecting contemporary Europe. They date from the time of the fall of the Berlin Wall, so are trends of the 1990s. I think the most worrying of them, especially for this audience, is a shift right across Europe towards insularity. This is perplexing and is something of a paradox; at a time of globalisation and proliferation of new broadcasting channels, to find this shift towards insularity, provincialism, and worse, xenophobia. Why is this the case? One reason is that with the advent of new channels, the competition between broadcasters, always fierce, has become vicious. What matters now is not the worth or purpose of the programme, but the audience share it commands. And with the rise of more channels comes the erosion of the audience-share each channel used to have. The rise of the commercial channel RTL in Holland has led to serious doubts as to the viability of the public service broadcaster in that country, while here in Britain the rise of BSkyB has been phenomenally successful commercially. Mr Murdoch has shown that British people are prepared to pay a subscription, which is, for television, an entirely new source of funding. So with the rise of these new channels, public service broadcasters especially find their audiences slipping.

What is the effect of this? Consider one area of programming by the BBC, roughly between 6.00 pm and 11.00 pm each day which we call peak time (I am picking a British broadcaster because being British myself I can be ruder about them at an international conference!). I conducted a study which involved examining the years from 1989 to 1994, and the coverage of one subject area, the Third World or southern hemisphere. In 1990, the BBC showed about 100 hours of programmes on this subject per year at peak time. As the decade progressed, this dropped very considerably. In fact, half of this window on the world shown by the BBC disappeared within five years. The BBC response to the Government's Green Paper promised a

'higher quality, a richer diversity and a broader choice of programmes, especially at peak time'. It is possible to sceptical about this.

However, the BBC was not alone. The four terrestrial channels,
especially the two popular channels, BBC1 and ITV, showed very few
of these kinds of programme in 1990 and now show even fewer, while
coverage on the minority channels, BBC2 and Channel 4, has
slumped considerably.

A last observation involves comparing documentaries and news. In
1991 and 1992 (the trend is the same in other years) if you wanted to
make it onto mainstream news, features dealing with conflict and war
would certainly get you there. More than half the coverage of the
southern hemisphere is about mayhem and war. The next-most covered subject is disasters: volcanic eruptions, earthquakes, famine and
so on. So virtually two-thirds of all coverage of the southern hemisphere would appear to show the inhabitants of that part of the world
in a particularly unflattering light. It's all mayhem and disorder. But
if you look at documentaries, you see a completely different trend.
Disaster and conflict account for only 10 per cent of these programmes, whereas the arts and culture account for much more. So
news and documentaries are complementary: news gives you a picture of world disasters, while documentaries show that it's a little
more complicated than that.

Why does this matter? I think it matters a great deal, because television news is the most influential of all the mass-media – that is what
the opinion polls suggest. During this expansion into new channels,
television news has retained its place in the schedules. For example,
the new Channel 5 news programme is shown at peak time; and there
is no question of displacing it. It may be more informal, but is basically the same thing. In fact, news is expanding. The BBC now broad-
casts a 24-hour news channel. I do not know who watchs this; perhaps
it is part of the BBC's world-wide ambitions, and it certainly costs a lot
of money. But it does show that television news is clearly holding its
place in the schedules.

In Europe the rise of xenophobia and 'fortress Europe' has actually generated headline news: about Albanian refugees clamouring
for access to Italy, asylum-seekers being shabbily treated, or violent
clashes about foreign immigrants in Belgium or Germany; these
almost nightly images project on a widespread scale a very threatening imagery to the settled indigenous cultures. The trend is thus one
of a proliferation of negative stories compared to the near exclusion
of counterbalancing pictures on mainstream television.

I would therefore argue that television news is reinforcing and inadvertently feeding xenophobia. It is certainly contributing to a lack of balance. We can see this most clearly with regard to the southern hemisphere. My organisation is of the view that when you see a picture of the Zeebrugge ferry disaster and the coverage it rightly claimed on our headline news, it will not stop you actually taking a ferry on holiday next week, because we know most ferries do not go to sea with their bow doors open. But our experience of other societies is so limited, apart from tourism, that we really have no idea of what normality is. The exceptional or the sensational becomes the norm. So, there is a paradox: at the very time the multichannel media seems to offer increased opportunities of cultural exchange, there is the danger that minority cultures will be overwhelmed. There have been a number of studies on this. One from Belgium, 'The Media and Multiculturalism in Flanders', asked people of Moroccan and Turkish origin what they thought of their portrayal on Belgian television. They thought coverage was at best sloppy and ill-informed, and in the coverage of religion, and social and political matters often quite unbalanced. In Denmark, which we think of as a model of enlightenment and internationalism, a study called 'Elite, Media and Minorities', produced by Copenhagen University, covered the years from 1985 when, it was claimed, Danish broadcasting subtly changed from a position of tolerance to one reflecting more the trends I've been describing. The study claimed that there was mass media stereotyping and manipulation of the portrayal of immigrants. In Germany, a well-known editor made a study last year of how foreigners were portrayed on German television. Italians were found to come across as pizza-makers and mafiosi, whereas most Italians living in Germany work in banks and other rather mundane occupations.

Am I painting a rather unfair picture of European broadcasters? At a policy level, it is accepted that there is a need for fair representation – this is so particularly with the more enlightened broadcasters, who tend to be, though they are not exclusively, public service broadcasters. They see it as a duty to take account of cultural minorities. For example, the BBC, in its policy document of last year, 'Extending Choice', names as one of its four key objectives the recognition of the full cultural diversity of this country. Channel 4 has a Multicultural Department and shows a staggering 130 hours of programmes each year, including documentaries, sitcoms, soaps and films, which reflect this diversity. In Sweden, SVT, the public service broadcaster, has agreed with the government that it has a 'major responsibility in

spreading the image of a multicultural Swedish society'. So, broadcasters are indeed responding to the needs of multicultural societies.

However, there is still in my view an awfully long way to go. One
problem is the lack of authoritative academic research. The only
book I have found on this issue is UNESCO's *Media and Cultural
Pluralism in Europe*, which looks at the record of each country. The
author concludes:

> We have seen that the television media in Europe is aware of the
> role it can and should play to promote cultural pluralism and com-
> bat racism and xenophobia. Each country and channel has chosen
> to do it in its own way. But what do migrants and minorities want in
> terms of programming?

In a bizarre way, this report illustrates that viewers have not been
asked how and what they do want to see and how they react to the
offer of programmes. But no proper study has been carried out on
this subject. Finally, there is the important issue of employing people
who belong to minority groups within the media; the same author
concludes that in no editorial department anywhere does the staff
faithfully represent the society in the country as a whole.

Several key things would thus appear necessary. Television needs to
represent the multiplicity of cultures in Europe today, and promote
the mutual respect which the other speakers at this conference have
mentioned. How is this to be done? A very useful seminar last year on
this matter has three key recommendations for broadcasters. One
was to increase the representation in the workforce of minorities,
both in front of, but also, and more importantly behind, the camera.
Some progress has been made in this country, where there are programmes very visibly reflecting the existence of minorities, although
in senior echelons of management this is not yet the case. A second
recommendation was to sensitise the workforce to the need for
greater minority representation. And it was finally recommended
that access be given to minorities so that their voices can be heard
within the mainstream, peak-time programmes.

I would add, in conclusion, that it is very important to move forward on some very practical initiatives. I think there is common
ground among broadcasters at the policy level, but what is missing in
so many cases is any real meat on the bone. This is, after all, the
European Year against Racism, though you would hardly know it.
There have, however, been some initiatives this year which are worthy

of praise. One, sponsored by the Council of Europe, was the 'Prize of Europe', an initiative of the 'One World' group of broadcasters, with the results to be screened across Europe later in the year, hosted by TV3, a Catalan channel in Spain with an enlightened stance on diversity. A second initiative has been a competition for young film-makers from minority backgrounds who have not had access to the airwaves, to make programmes that will be guaranteed a screening. Finally there has been the BBC's 'Race in the Frame' series. I made a programme for this and discovered that on 'The Generation Game', one of the BBC's most popular ever peak-time Saturday entertainment programmes, only three black couples have appeared in 25 years of the show.

So, for those of you interested in a more detailed examination of the issues, I will either recommend this series to you – or suggest we meet for a drink in the bar afterwards.

THE COLD EYE

Malachi O'Doherty

The camera searches for the details of our lives. The people behind it seek to package those details into coherent presentations of how things are. That is the simple assessment of what is going on when the media comes into our world. We all know that the media changes that world just by being in it. The anthropologist tiptoeing through the islands of the South Pacific was unable to maintain the conceit that she was merely a watcher. In physics, the watcher is the element which comprises every conclusion. That is Heisenberg's uncertainty principle. How do you watch and at the same time compensate for the fact of your being there? You cannot.

Walk the length of the Falls Road in Belfast with a camera and you will be flocked by the children of the most closely observed people in the country. They want their picture taken. You will get knowing looks from their parents. They are fed up with the scrutiny. They react to foreign journalists as if they have known them since before they came. Yet people in the media hold jealously to their imagined objectivity. It is almost a spiritual principle for them. Two things they find difficult to accept are, that they rarely see the real world, if there is a real world, and that whatever they touch they change. In 1970 the press carried the first picture of a teenage girl who had been tarred and feathered by the IRA for dating a British soldier. The image was a warning to other women to stay away from social events organised by the army. Was the photographer not part of the machinery for conveying that message? Indeed, would there have been any point in punishing the girl in a public place, if the photographer had not been there to relay the message? Did the punishers wait until the photographer arrived?

When the UDA drilled on the streets of North Belfast, they provided a similar image for the press, a man stripped to the waist and tied to a post. A placard declared that he was a thief. A very simple means of getting the media to serve the objectives of the paramilitaries had been discovered and passed on.

A lone gunman, Michael Stone attacked the funeral of three IRA members when it arrived at Milltown Cemetery in West Belfast and gathered around the open graves. His apparent intention was to kill mourners, as many as possible. He was armed with a Browning nine-millimetre automatic pistol and a cache of stun grenades. That is to say, he was ill-equipped for the task in hand. With hundreds of people packed close together at the graveside he managed to kill only three. At least one of those was shot in close pursuit of Stone as he ran away. Yet Stone became a kind of paramilitary star. The jacket he wore was raffled in a loyalist club. What made his blundering rampage significant was that it was visible. The cameras had been there for the funeral, and they turned to watch this little curly-haired man, in a cloth cap and anorak, trundle his way through the graves, pursued by dozens of furious men, then turning to pock-pock at them blithely with his pistol, as if he was tossing sweets to scrambling urchins. Stone's demeanour is the puzzle. He did not move like a man who believed that this was real. It was more like pantomime. It was as if he imagined himself to be on a stage that he was free to step off. Millions gaped in awe at him over tea that night on television. For them it was real and shocking. Stone was performing, insulated from the implications of what he was doing in the real world by its meaning in the world of the watcher. Did he know that he was on television? Was it his own indulgence for the camera that made possible for him a lunacy with a semblance of courage?

Four days later the camera was on hand for another calamity. This was different. There was no showman this time. The cameras had come to see the funeral of one of the men Michael Stone had killed. Suddenly a car confronted the funeral. There were screeches of tyres. The driver tried to reverse. A black taxi blocked his way. The crowd, fearing another attack, swarmed onto the car. A man inside produced a pistol and fired a shot. The crowd suddenly divided into four. One group launched a more methodical attack on the car. Another became stewards. That group restrained the third group, the main body of the crowd, which included people who wanted a closer look or to join in. The camera crews were a fourth group, watching everything. The stewards rushed about to try to stop the filming, to protect the squad attacking the car from that probing cold eye, which would not judge this as anything but interesting. The two men in the car turned out to be soldiers, and a small group captured them, stripped them, questioned them, and shot them dead.

After that incident, many of the people who swarmed over the car were prosecuted. The footage of their behaviour became evidence. The police demanded access to it. This raised, in a very practical way, the question of whether the cold eye could regard itself as uninvolved. The independence of the camera was defended on pragmatic rather than principled grounds. For their own safety, crews had to be trusted not to be working for the state against paramilitaries. If that independence could not be asserted in this case, crews at future disturbances would be at risk of attack from those who saw them as a potential ally of the police. Usually the camera does not get close enough to the action to be implicated in it. More commonly, it comes along afterwards, to see the charred building, or the body on the road, with a sheet already draped over it. Sometimes it has only the evidence of long memories available to it.

Who knows what happened to Jean McConville, kidnapped by the IRA, with no witnesses but her children, now grown up, to piece together the story. One daughter Helen, talking to About Face Media Productions, recalls the broken promises of social workers and the temper of a nun, more vividly than the callousness of the men who took their mother away.

The memories of women from the Shankill and the Falls, collated for Marcia Rock's 'Daughters of the Troubles', trawl the past for another explanation of division, the priorities of the hard world of men. This seems almost confirmed in the slick propaganda of the Northern Ireland Office. 'Cat In the Cradle' is a compressed drama of a young paramilitary killer ageing to disillusionment, while his sons grow up to join a new generation of gunmen. The target audience of this film was presumably the middle-aged killers themselves, who might at least now salvage a life for their children if they have nothing else to show for their barbarous ways. Yet the film seems to glamorise the gun and the certainties of brash physicality. Whatever for? To be all the more plausible to the type of people addressed by it? Yet it has all the stock attractions of a thriller, and seems dangerously close to selling the merits of being able to handle a gun. Drama approaches the history of Irish division with the same risk of inadvertently taking sides. The past is trimmed to be a weapon for various communal interests. That means that anyone, like the producers of the BBC's 'The Hanging Gale', who seeks to recreate a period like that of the Irish famine, may be regarded as passing judgement on the choices made by political leaders of today.

In the ferment of social change today, drama treads sensitive ground too. The success of the BBC series 'Ballykissangel', the story

of the priest's developing friendship with a young woman, lies partly
in that it resonates with current Irish anxieties about the sexuality of
Catholic clergy. A priest who has the freedom to fall in love is a much
more reassuring image today than it was only ten years ago. Once
viewers would have felt only anxiety for the man's moral welfare. A
new generation believes that if only the priests were allowed to be
happy, the whole of society would be enriched – and better protected
against the sexual predators who have skulked among them.

With the new technology, people have less need simply to wait and
see what the cold eye makes of them. They have the freedom now to
explore the potential of the media as a means of reflecting their own
smaller community back to itself, or for exploring their differences
with others. That can work two ways. Community groups may use
media skills to help people express themselves, or they may try to con-
vey a message to a select audience. The two approaches can not be
wholly separated out from each other, but clearly the little animated
film by Filmation, of baying sheep declaring their territory, as a par-
ody of the stand-offs between Orange parades and protesters, was primarily an exercise in bringing children to see that both sides of the
argument have much in common. Educators have tried to involve
children in more sophisticated films, to act out and illustrate prejudice and its problems. So a Protestant boy pleads with a girl for
another date. Last time he got into a fight with 'Fenian bastards'. It
was their fault. She surely understands that. It is the question of what
he would understand that is left hanging in the air.

The cold eye of the camera is neither neutral nor objective, but it
is distant, and it seems oblivious to the ways in which it influences the
events it records. Often those who face the camera are much more
aware of the influence it can have. When reporters went to Harryville
in Ballymena to observe the loyalist picket of a Catholic church, the
protesters abused and berated them, regarding the camera as their
enemy. It might be tempting for broadcasters in a divided society to
imagine that giving equal offence to both sides confirms their neu-
trality. That is one of the comforting myths of people in the media;
they tell themselves that they must be getting something right if both
parties to a quarrel blame them. It is not so simple.

Those loyalists at Harryville regarded the camera as serving Irish
nationalism, while nationalists at the funeral at which two soldiers
were attacked and killed, feared it for a wholly different reason, that
it might simply expose dirty work. The resistance of those the camera
points at, can also affirm the media's sense that it is doing good work,

exposing that which others would hide. The danger is that in representing the hidden and the appalling it might purport to be representing society as a whole. We need to be alert to what it misses.

The cold eye of the camera can get in the way, but it can also
become now, a tool in the hands of minorities and sectional interests
with something to say. It strains to explain us to ourselves. It does not
always get it wrong.

CULTURAL EDUCATION OF YOUNG PEOPLE AND THE NEED TO PRESERVE IDENTITY IN A UNITED EUROPE

Jerzy Chmiel and Ewa Repsch

The pupils of today will celebrate their maturity in a Europe and a world inhabited by nations and states united to a greater extent than they are today. For Europe there exists no better solution. The process of integration is enhanced by a number of civilisation-related factors, and attracts much attention on the part of international organisations, while various communities in particular countries become involved and act in favour of the whole process. The belief that the survival of humanity depends on the readiness of nations and states to unite, becomes more and more commonly shared; only then will it become possible for them to face the emerging threats. But for similar beliefs to become commonly shared, and for the coming generations to become capable of creating a united world and of living in it, it is necessary to prepare young people properly. At present, this seems to be one of the leading and most demanding tasks in the sphere of education.

Culture is one of the most important components of many educational programmes, involving all the complexity resulting from history, tradition, manners and related paradigms of emotional life, and attitudes towards peoples' own countries and other nations and states. It is important to take advantage of the existing diversity, to appreciate equally the home-grown and the unique which characterise particular cultures, and to rely on them for integration, so that they help people to recognise the strength of diversity in unity.

Such is the understanding of cultural education and conservation of cultural heritage among the intellectual elites of Europe, expressed in their incentives both in the sphere of international co-operation and cross-regional cultural exchange. Moral support and guidance, which will illustrate similar modes of thinking, are contained in declarations, adopted by such international organisations as the UN or UNESCO, and also in numerous documents and addresses.

Organisational and programme-based solutions adopted in the Polish educational system, also encourage a cultural education influenced by the ideas of preservation of cultural identity, and openness to other cultures. In recent years, a whole system of language courses and colleges has been set up in order to enhance mutual understanding. The number of students is constantly growing, and so is the number of schools and educational and fostering centres taking part in contests designed to test knowledge of Europe, such as the European School Competition, where in the last five years the number of participants increased from a few hundred to 35,000 (in 1996). European Clubs have been established in many schools, and in several hundred schools the programme designed to bring young people closer to the European Community is being implemented. Culture plays an essential role in this movement. Numerous international festivals, organised both by Poland and by other countries, with the participation of artistic groups and ensembles composed of schoolchildren and of individual pupils, along with cross-regional exchange in the sphere of culture (involving regions, schools, particular school forms), offer the possibility of promoting both the culture of a given country, and also openness to, learning about, and harmony with other cultures. Another wonderful opportunity is offered by European camp meetings designed for young people who share similar interests or are winners in particular types of contests. This form of activity, which is new for Polish youth, evokes a tremendous interest in school-related circles, and all the reports by participants prove that it is extremely valuable from a purely educational point of view.

An important step towards awarding the proper place, significance, and definition of the role of cultural heritage in the didactic and child-rearing process, in the context of European and world culture, was marked by presenting Polish schools in 1995 with programme guidelines entitled 'Cultural Heritage at the Regional Level'. That document, which proves so very modern, stems from the traditional approach, manifested in the Polish pedagogical tradition as early as the 17th century by Amos Komensky, who wrote that becoming acquainted not just with the world, but primarily his or her immediate surroundings, was a child's natural right. Though the guidelines remain well-rooted in the education traditions, their legal basis is provided by the Educational System Act of 7 September 1991, which states: 'Education . . . serves the purposes of developing in youth, a sense of responsibility, love for Motherland and respect for the Polish cultural heritage, accompanied by openness to values represented by various cultures of Europe and the world'. Such a clause in a piece of source legislation which constitutes the basis of the didactic and child-rearing system, best illustrates the changes which are taking place in Poland.

The purpose of 'Cultural Heritage at the Regional Level', designed to be implemented in the course of the didactic process, is to strengthen in pupils their sense of identity, and encourage both their involvement in the functioning of their own community and their genuine opening to other communities and cultures. The document assumes the need to furnish a pupil with a certain body of knowledge about his or her own region in connection with the broad context of realities of life at the national, and even international, level, taking into account various planes of the regional environment, and stressing, in the course of the educational process, manifold values traditionally cultivated in each region, recognising them on the national, state and human scale. The point is to shape a pupil's identity not in isolation but by way of creating open, liberal, tolerant attitudes oriented towards acknowledging and understanding the pluralism of various existing cultures.

'Cultural Heritage at the Regional Level' contains programme guidelines. Hence, it is possible to use that document in each school, community or region. It indicates the scope of issues, defines aims and imposes a certain order, prompting contents and methods, inspiring forms and limiting the freedom to pick and choose on the basis of local traditions. Related decisions are left to be made by teachers, schools and all other community-based participants in the process of education. Programme guidelines are designed to inspire, but not to impose particular solutions in a centralistic manner. They are not designed to manage, either. The principle that the contents of the educational process assume reconciling the regional and the universal, in order to solve possible social, ethnic and religious conflicts, teach mutual respect, and restore traditional, timeless values, preparing people for a rewarding participation in the life of the uniting Europe, is very strongly articulated. Programme guidelines were designed as an instrument of modern national education, stemming from regional cultural heritage, which means the possibility of shifting the focus from the personal and the regional to the national and all-human. The guidelines are designed to integrate, covering regional culture, without referring to particular subjects. They constitute a consistent teaching bloc, assuming continuity from the kindergarten level though subsequent stages in school education, and indicate didactic and other out-of-school activities, certainly applying diversified working methods, and the necessity of engaging with the wider environment surrounding the school (represented by artistic associations, regional associations, and others).

Annexes constitute an integral part of the document; they build on the programme guidelines and contribute to their significance. They include:

1. 'Charter of Polish Regionalism', passed by the fifth Congress of Regional Cultural Associations in 1994. This Charter remains absolutely consistent with objectives, assumptions and notions contained in 'Cultural Heritage at the Regional Level';

2. 'Recommendation on the Safeguarding of Traditional Folklore and Culture' adopted at the 25th General Conference of UNESCO on 15 November 1989 in Paris, which recognises folklore and folk art as components of the world heritage of humanity and a powerful instrument to unite people and communities;

3. Final documents of the Conference of the UN on Environment and Development, adopted in June 1992 in Rio de Janeiro (short version) which recommend balanced development of regions;

4. 'International Charter of Geographical Education' (short version) which stresses the right to full geographical education aimed at balancing regional and national identity with thinking in terms of international and global perspectives.

Actions initiated in the Polish educational system are aimed at restoring due importance to region-based didactic activities, giving a chance of gaining proper acquaintance with the local culture and historical heritage in order to make citizens more conscious of their capacities and commitments to their country, and their 'small homeland', more open and willing to understand other cultures and to participate in European co-operation.

INTERPRETING CULTURAL DIVERSITY FOR MUTUAL UNDERSTANDING

ARTISTS, SCHOOLS AND INTERCULTURALISM

John Van Santen

A decade ago we were celebrating the Australian Bicentenary in Britain. Schools, television and the media generally gave extensive coverage to the occasion and in London we saw a range of Australian exhibitions including a show of Aboriginal Australian art. All this stimulated primary schools throughout the country to take up the Australian theme with their children, and we became aware of the great richness of the Australian cultural heritage. Many of the extraordinary animals seemed almost to have been designed for children. The geographical and climatic conditions showed themselves to be strikingly varied. Even much of the history of the country seemed to be within the grasp of young children in Britain. In addition this celebration introduced us to the Aboriginals whose art we found so appealing and whose way of life was oft presented as somewhat romantic and exotic. Many teachers though, quite rightly perceived the Aboriginals as an ethnic minority facing cultural destruction and they sought ways of helping the children to find out something about these people.

I remember this time especially well as I was trying to discover something about how children and teachers were responding to the galleries and educational resources of the Commonwealth Institute in London. Talking to these teachers and pupils gave me a number of intriguing insights into the situation of people trying to gain understanding of cultures of which they had no experience. I shall give two examples.

The first concerns a ten-year-old boy from Northampton, 60 miles north of London, who with his class had travelled to the Commonwealth Institute in London to carry out a class project on Australia. He had asked his teacher if they were going to pass through Dover, which lies some 60 miles south-east of London. His teacher had several times shown him the geographical relationship of these three towns on a map, but this proved beyond his level of abstraction.

And yet he was expected to deal with concepts involving a culture from the other side of the world. The second example is of a teacher whose class was fascinated by Aboriginal paintings made up of masses of black and white dots. Her main concern was how her pupils could reproduce the dots without spending too much time. These stories show some of the problems faced by multiculturalism.

The example of the boy from Northampton shows a possible mismatch between intercultural learning expectations and the conceptual development of young children. Australia is now seen as an unsuitable source of learning projects as there are really no opportunities for first-hand learning experiences, to build on their own experiences of the world. This is not seen as desirable until children have reached what Piaget called the formal-operational stage of thinking.

A decade ago, when these examples occurred, already some experiments suggested that children were capable of recognising intentions in others at an age earlier than Piaget thought possible.[1] Children often see images of other cultures on television, as though that medium confers a sense of reality on what is being seen. Also, today many more children do travel abroad, thus gaining first-hand experiences of other cultures.

But the second example I gave poses not a problem of psychological perception, but a range of questions about art education, whether about the techniques employed by the Aboriginal painters, or the social or cultural significance of the images created. The answers to these questions could have formed the basis of a worthwhile practical work, where the expectation would not be that the result would look like an Aboriginal painting. The search for the answers to the questions raised in these examples leads to the wider sphere of the setting of art into a social and cultural context, in doing so bringing to us the problem of trying to help children gain understanding of another culture with which they have had no first-hand contact.

In 1987 the Artists and Craftspeople in Education (ACE) Project was formed at the International Centre for Intercultural Studies at the University of London. The object of the project was to find ways of helping pupils of all ages and their teachers to overcome the sort of difficulties I have described. At the moment, the Project has worked with more than 60 schools, with pupils of all ages, backgrounds and abilities. Third-level students have also been involved. Groups of these young people work with carefully selected artists from outside the European tradition – usually spending about a week with them. The broad intentions of the Project are that, first, all students and teachers should have the chance to learn about the processes involved in the making of art, and second, that they should develop their own intercultural understanding while doing this. The ACE Project works closely with schools prior to the week in which the artist will be involved – this ensures thorough preparation, and teachers are helped to set the work in the context of the wider curriculum. After the workshop week the Project will continue to help broaden the experience within the school. Although the primary purpose is thorough engagement with the process of making art, the work is always exhibited to a professional standard in a gallery of some distinction. Artists' work will be displayed alongside that of the pupils. Some work has been shown in the British Museum, the Museum of Mankind and the Museum of London.

Part of the artist's task is to introduce children to relevant cultural influences on their own artistic development. A Ugandan artist told one child, who asked him why he became an artist, that there is in his language no word for artist and that he was a skilled craftsman like any other, who learned by watching people at work in his village. Children on the Project were able to gain a rich insight into the artist's home culture through anecdotes, books, tapes, and explanations of the meaning of their work. This was set against the contemporary context of the artist's working life in this country, and the sources of current creative ideas.

Let me now try to give some idea of what these projects are like.[2] The first one I shall describe was inspired by the 'Arts of Hinduism' exhibition in the British Museum in 1993–94. This week-long project involved a group of six- and seven-year-old children from an infants' school in London working with the ACE project and the artist Sue Lovell.

On the first day, the children were introduced to the exhibition's rich variety of paintings, textiles and temple sculptures by a member of the British Museum Education Service. They also heard some of the stories surrounding the lives of the principal Hindu gods and goddesses. The children then embarked on several drawing tasks, starting with drawing each other in Indian clothes. They were asked to find and draw as many images as they could find of temples, and also of facial expressions, hands, feet, chariots, rivers or trees. They then made drawings of animals in the exhibition. Finally they made drawing of shrines and altars.

On the second day, Sue Lovell showed the children some of her own sketch books and constructed paintings or icon boxes and she described to them how she works. The children each chose a box from a selection of small wine and cigar boxes and began to prepare surfaces with size before pasting on photocopies of their drawings. They also learned to mix and apply gesso to some of the surfaces. On the next day the children were introduced to plaster casting and made casts from small treasured objects or other available small figures. They continued with the application of gesso and some of them made additional doors for their boxes. They also started to use watercolour on their photocopied drawings. By the end of the following day they had completed the making, casting, painting and varnishing of the three-dimensional figures. On the day after that, these were arranged and fixed in the boxes, the painting was completed and the 'shrine boxes' finished with a coat of varnish.

These children had the rare experience of spending a whole week on a single project with a professional artist. They worked in two and three dimensions using a wide variety of materials and they learned something about the art and mythology of Hinduism.

The inspiration for the second example was an exhibition of Japanese prints, The Passionate Art of Utaramo at the British Museum in 1996. On this occasion a group of 17-year-old girls from a London school worked with the sculptor Juginder Lamba to produce their own blocks and prints. Again the students were introduced to the work of Utaramo in the context of 18th-century Tokyo. They also had opportunities to draw each other wearing Japanese clothes. This gave them a means of looking at Utaramo's images of women with more interest and understanding.

The students were asked to spend two hours making drawings for the exhibition. They concentrated on figures, patterns and the characteristic Japanese interest in diagonals, both architectural and in interiors. By the beginning of the first afternoon they had enough material to start working on ideas for the block design. Each student was given a block of prepared oak and adopted the Japanese method of starting to work in red ink, then working over the design in black as the ideas were refined and problems resolved. By the end of the first day they had pasted the completed designs face-down onto the blocks. The following morning the paste had dried and the design no longer visible as it was on the underside of the block. The Japanese method of rubbing paper with a little vegetable oil makes the paper transparent, and the design shows through clearly. When the block is cut the design is reversed but prints taken from it are consistent with the original design.

The next task was learning how to use a variety of chisels and gouges with heavy mallets on wood with largely unknown properties. The students soon realised that there was an enormous amount of detailed work to be done. This required concentration and was physically very demanding. Two days were spent carving and many of the completed blocks showed a remarkable degree of controlled detail. The final days were spent printing and this too became an experimental and varied experience. They worked with papers of different weights in a range of colours using a nipping press.

The production of colour woodblock prints in Japan involved a chain of people with highly developed skills and expertise. An artist produced a design which was then given to a blockcutter. For colour prints a separate block was cut from each colour, which might have required the making of 20 or more blocks for any one print. The task of printing was then passed on to a specialist printer. This project involved the use of only one colour, black, and so only a single block was necessary. Nevertheless these students experienced all three of these fields of technical and aesthetic skill. The students also had the rare experience of working with a distinguished sculptor for a week. They learned something of how he works, his exacting standards and the constant stream of decisions which must be made every day. The enthusiasm and commitment of these students enabled them to become involved in the process and discipline of making art to a high standard, and it brought them closer to culture.

The young people working on these projects had worked with, and as, artists for the duration of the week. It was therefore fitting that their work should be professionally exhibited and in both cases the finished work together with many of the preparatory drawings was exhibited in the British Museum.

To conclude, we need to return to the art education problem and the conceptual development problem which emerged with the visits to the Commonwealth Institute. We can begin with the art education problem indicated by the teacher who wanted to know the best way of getting the children to do the dots so that their paintings looked as much as possible like Aboriginal paintings. Might she have been helped by the experience of either of the projects I have described? I hope so. The group of infants who made the 'shrine boxes' in response to the Hinduism exhibition were not trying to make a facsimile of anything in the exhibition. They were using their drawings and other skills learned during the week to create very personal responses to the idea of Hindu shrines. They were helped to gain understanding of Hindu gods and goddesses through stories and particular drawing tasks. The planning and practice of any piece of art work can be ambitious without being beyond the competencies of the children.

The other problem was raised by the boy from Northampton who could not grasp the geographical relationship between his own town, London and Dover, but was expected to make sense of a project on Australia. How might he have fared on a project such as those I have described?

I would like to think that the level of intense involvement for a full week would have enabled him to form some kind of lasting connection. Perhaps he would have found that as a result of the experience he could not walk past an art exhibition without wondering how the exhibits were made, what materials had been used, how long it had taken, what social significance the object had for the maker. Working with the art of another culture in a sustained way with the need to complete the work by the end of he week leads to the development of a powerful sense of commitment and enthusiasm. Becoming immersed in the processes of making art and in the art of another culture may, we hope, enable young people to contribute more to their own multicultural society.

NOTES

1. See for example M. Donaldson, *Children's Minds* (London, Fontana, 1978).
2. Slides were shown of work in progress and finished work.

EDUCATION FOR MUTUAL UNDERSTANDING IN THE NORTHERN IRELAND CURRICULUM: POLICIES, PROGRESS AND PROBLEMS

Vivien McIver

Introduction

I find myself sandwiched between two very engaging sessions this morning, doomed to give you what amounts to a history lesson. You have just heard Alan Smith tell it 'like it is', warts and all, about Education for Mutual Understanding (EMU), and I am to be followed by my colleague in the Inspectorate, Liz Armour, who will introduce you to the broad sunlit uplands of the European Studies project. My session will, I fear, be rather less titillating: indeed, having heard what was said about the thrills and spills of trying to implement EMU in Northern Ireland, you could be forgiven for thinking that EMU (and all of us associated with it over so many years) now find ourselves standing, shaken and bedraggled, on the shore of a Pool of Tears, like poor Alice and the mouse, the Lory, and the other creatures in that episode in *Alice's Adventures in Wonderland*. My history lesson this morning may be just about as effective as that of the mouse on that occasion in helping them all to dry out! You may recall that his history lesson ran as follows:

> 'Ahem!' said the Mouse with an important air. 'Are you all ready? This is the driest thing I know. Silence all round if you please! "William the Conqueror, whose cause was favoured by the Pope, was soon submitted to by the English, who wanted leaders, and had been of late much accustomed to usurpation and conquest. Edwin and Morcar, the Earls of Mercia and Northumbria – " '
> 'Ugh!' said the Lory, with a shiver.[1]

I hope my history lesson is not as dry (if not exactly drying!) as that, but why give it at all? We get many visitors to Northern Ireland who

come explicitly to learn about our attempt to introduce EMU into
our curriculum, and to draw on our experience prior to introducing
something like EMU into their own education systems. You may be
here for the same reason, and if this history lesson about EMU helps
you to do that, it will have served its purpose. But be under no illu-
sion! It is a lesson, and like all good lessons, it finishes with a demanding test – you see the lengths to which I am prepared to go to keep
you awake!

Origins

Not men and women in an Irish street
But Catholics and Protestants you meet

These lines were written over 100 years ago by the Ulster poet William
Allingham; they do not tell the whole story, but they capture
something fundamental about past and present divisions in
Northern Ireland. More important to the issue we are addressing
here they tell us something also about the need for, and to an extent
the origins of, Education for Mutual Understanding (EMU) in our
divided society. Ireland has always had divisions; as a consequence
it has always had wounds in need of healing and since the advent
of public education in the 19th century there have been those
who have seen education as one way of attempting to heal them.
One of the giants of Irish education in the 19th century, PW Joyce,
wrote:

> I have tried to write this history book soberly and moderately,
> avoiding exaggeration and bitterness, pointing to extenuating cir-
> cumstances . . . giving credit where credit is due and showing fair
> play all round. Perhaps this book, written, I hope, in a broad and
> just spirit, may help to foster mutual feelings of respect and
> toleration among Irish people of different parties and may teach
> them to love and admire what is great and noble in their history, no
> matter where found.[2]

Joyce wrote this in the 1890s so, you see, Education for Mutual
Understanding (though not called by that name) has long been an
aspiration in Irish education.

If we turn to more recent times, I think it might be useful to
explain the process by which EMU has found a permanent place in

the new curriculum of Northern Ireland schools. In doing so I want to indicate who I see as the prime movers, those who make things happen (for better or worse I will leave you to judge) in an education system which, like most established systems, is healthily sceptical of change. I should also emphasise from the outset that all of this is a highly personal view.

Schools – oases of calm or catalysts for change?

The Northern Ireland school system is largely segregated. This means that Catholic children attend Catholic schools; Protestant children attend state schools which, although non-denominational, are predominantly Protestant. At the beginning of the present period of violence over 20 years ago the majority of teachers prided themselves on maintaining normality for children in their classrooms and in their schools as the world around them was shaken by civil unrest. Schools were seen as 'oases of calm' to be protected at all costs from the violence outside their gates. But there were also some teachers, small in number but growing steadily through the 1970s, who were determined that education should make some contribution to the solution to the problem and not just, as they saw it, remain a part of it. History teachers were in the vanguard of this development. Teaching in the segregated circumstances I have described earlier, the history teachers came together to discuss how they were tackling the thorny issue of teaching Irish history with a view to ensuring that they were not teaching the subject in any biased way on whichever side of the religious divide they taught. These contacts led directly to the development of new materials for teaching Irish history which emphasised a careful scrutiny of the nature of historical evidence and which were written jointly by Catholic and Protestant teachers for use in schools of all kinds. Some teachers from other disciplines soon followed the history teachers' lead and the links forged between individual teachers, Protestant and Catholic, led in some cases, to regular contacts between schools and classes and children. But at this stage in the 1970s and early 1980s this coming together was limited in scale, and depended on the commitment and enthusiasm of individual teachers and individual schools. There was some government support from the Northern Ireland Department of Education but this tended to be in response to particular requests rather than being set aside for the purpose. This in effect represented a benign but otherwise neutral response to EMU.

The seminal years

Enthusiasm can be a waning asset especially in the troubled circumstances in which schools found themselves in Northern Ireland in the
early years of the Troubles. What the small-scale funding served to do
was to keep the flame of teacher enthusiasm for EMU alive in this
period of uncertainty and experimentation. Indeed there was a sizeable number of the teacher enthusiasts who wanted nothing more
than this from 'officialdom' for too much support from a branch of
government could be counter-productive, could come with too many
strings attached and could be off-putting for one side or the other in
a divided state. Despite these sensitivities and difficulties, this period
proved to be an important stage in the history of EMU. On the face
of it though, progress 'on the ground' was slow and unspectacular –
a circular signalling the Department's commitment to improving
community relations through schools; some small-scale funding for
joint work between schools; exhortation and a little funding to our
five Education and Library Boards to support EMU activities (but
only if the local authorities so wished) and the setting up of an EMU
committee – these represented the main stimuli for EMU during this
period.

    Nevertheless the policy, however frail, worked reasonably well. The
Department's circular mentioned above was entitled 'The
Improvement of Community Relations: the contribution of schools'
and stated very clearly that:

> Our education system has clearly a vital role to play in the task of
> fostering improved relationships between the two communities in
> Northern Ireland. Every teacher, every school manager, Board
> member and trustee, and every educational administrator within
> the system has a responsibility for helping children to learn to
> understand and respect each other, and their differing customs
> and traditions, and of preparing them to live together in harmony
> in adult life.

This level of official endorsement was valued by those involved in
EMU who felt they had been labouring in the wilderness up to this
point, and some of the education and library boards took EMU very
much to heart, with one in particular making very significant progress.

    Likewise the newly established EMU committee proved to be an
influential group not only for what it did in the early stages but also
for providing a forum where all those interested in promoting EMU

could meet regularly. Its members came from so many different back-grounds and starting points that they had much to discuss and much to resolve before they could hope to move forward together. For example, they had to agree on a definition of EMU to which all could subscribe. After much debate this definition included the need for children and young people:

◻ to learn to respect and value themselves and other people;
◻ to know about and value both their own culture and traditions, and those of others with different culture and traditions;
◻ to learn the importance of resolving differences and conflict by peaceful and creative means.

This process too was both successful and necessary for future developments.

All this time, however, as far as the wider education world in Northern Ireland was concerned, EMU still remained, comparatively speaking, somewhat mysterious and, perhaps because of this, even questionable in some quarters. Those most actively concerned in EMU considered it best done quietly without publicity or fuss so as to avoid upsetting others less favourably disposed. In the end, the EMU committee did appoint two field officers to help schools who wished to introduce EMU programmes, and the committee also produced a 'Teachers Guide to EMU'. All that was done in a spirit of 'don't rock the boat' and 'steady as we go'. Nevertheless, with hindsight, the EMU committee laid sound foundations and proved to be possibly the most seminal body in a seminal period.

Man with a mission

The quiet, limited approach changed quite dramatically with the advent of a new Minister for Education for Northern Ireland. This minister took office in the mid-1980s and almost immediately took up EMU with a degree of almost evangelical zeal. He was determined to bring the whole issue out into the open and to make it the concern of all in education. His approach was direct; his avowed intention was to place EMU at the heart of the Northern Ireland curriculum as the fourth 'R' with the role of improving 'Relationships' among young people. His positive espousal of EMU was welcomed by some, scepti-cally received by others, resisted by not a few. To have strong ministe-rial backing has both a positive and negative side.

In general, the minister met with considerable success. There had always been two main strands to EMU – that which took place *within* a school and that which took place *between* Catholic and state schools. In the first instance, the minister was particularly keen to encourage purposeful contact between schools across the religious divide in Northern Ireland and to that end he inaugurated the 'Cross-Community Contact Scheme'. The purpose of the Scheme was simple enough – to encourage schools to bring Catholic and Protestant children together on a regular basis so that they would get to know one another and form friendships through working together on aspects of the curriculum. The funding the minister provided was attractive and the criteria for getting it relatively simple to meet – if two or more schools, Catholic and Protestant, decided to work together on any aspect of the curriculum they would receive funds from the Department of Education provided they agreed to meet regularly, share a curricular task and needed to collaborate actively to complete that task. The result was that the cross-community aspect of EMU took off. The Department was inundated by proposals for joint work between Catholic and Protestant schools and it is interesting to note that this has since developed to the point where over one-third of all schools in Northern Ireland are now engaged in joint work.

The other aspect is EMU within schools. This was dealt with quite differently for whereas contact between schools across the religious divide was, and remains, entirely voluntary, EMU within schools has become a legal requirement in the new statutory Northern Ireland curriculum. This means that it is compulsory for all teachers to make provision for EMU as an educational theme permeating all subjects in the curriculum within every school.

EMU – voluntary or compulsory?

I will pause here to ask which approach to EMU is better – 'voluntary' or 'compulsory'? (Indeed the latter could be seen, and is so by some, as something of a contradiction in terms!) There would have been some obvious major difficulties if EMU *between* schools had been made compulsory. The location of some schools in Northern Ireland and the circumstances in which they find themselves would make it difficult, if not impossible, for them to find a partner school with which to work. As well as these practical realities, it is surely the case that, if we are to hope for beneficial outcomes, working contact between schools should not be forced, but is best encouraged between those schools and teachers who wish to undertake it.

There would be some equally serious difficulties if EMU *within* schools were left as a voluntary activity. Not least of these is the fact that the whole of the school curriculum is now set out in law, and is therefore a statutory requirement. If an aspect of it (eg EMU) were not to be statutory, it would run the risk of being ignored by busy teachers. That is not to minimise the problems a compulsory policy can create. When every teacher in Northern Ireland must, by statute, promote EMU how well will this highly sensitive matter be dealt with by the reluctant or ill-equipped teacher? Might he or she not do more harm than good? But education must always proceed with a degree of faith!

On balance then it is probably true that in both instances the right decision was taken. To make EMU between schools compulsory would have been impractical and possibly counter-productive. To leave EMU within school as a voluntary activity when the government was putting in place a statutory curriculum would have been to marginalise EMU and could have led to its extinction.

The minister's robust intervention and direct support for EMU brought about a highly significant change which still bears testimony to the effect that someone in such a position can have on what was, until then, a novel, peripheral, rather 'maverick' aspect of education. The other side of the coin also bears examination; such overt espousal of a cause such as EMU by a government minister can meet with considerable resistance from various quarters which may, or may not, be connected with the nature of the cause itself.

Whatever the origins of opposition to EMU it certainly arouses passionate feelings both for and against, and at this stage it may be useful to consider the nature of some of the opposition. As I have said earlier, some of the opposition can simply be a reaction to it as a ministerial initiative, but some is argued on more educational grounds. In the latter case, the whole development is seen as a misuse of the school curriculum for ends which are not considered genuinely educational; EMU is thus seen as a waste of children's time, a contrivance doomed to failure since it is quite unreasonable to expect school children to succeed, in terms of developing better relationships across the religious divide, where adults have manifestly failed. Less rational, more emotional and so still more vehemently argued is another viewpoint that EMU is a plot designed to condition children, to capture by stealth their hearts and minds and turn them into unionists or nationalists depending on which side is leading the attack on EMU at any particular time.

Catching the tide

External circumstances can not only alter cases but also favour causes. Towards the end of the 1980s, the increasing emphasis on matters European helped the EMU cause. For, in this regard, common citizenship of the new Europe proved to be a common bond among young people in a divided society like ours. Catholics in Northern Ireland consider themselves, in the main, to be Irish; Protestants consider themselves, in the main, to be British. These are firmly, deeply and sincerely held convictions with very strong historical roots. But, whatever divides them, our young people, Catholic and Protestant, from Northern Ireland or the Republic of Ireland, now share common citizenship of the new Europe. It is in this European context that they can relax with one another and discuss and examine their similarities and differences, and also the challenges they now share as young Europeans. So it is in the context of Europe that we have set some of our EMU joint work projects. Educationalists in Northern Ireland would be foolish not to capitalise on the circumstance of the spirit of co-operation in Europe to promote EMU. We would also be foolish not to 'catch the tide' or, in other words, tap into the national and international internet in EMU (borne out by a Conference such as this one) as other people in other places try to grapple with the contribution education can have to improving relationships, and cultural diversity.

'How stands the good old cause?'

How 'good' are our EMU activities? What 'good' is EMU doing? How do we measure cause and effect? Efficiency and effectiveness? The Department of Education in Northern Ireland monitors some of these aspects of EMU through its Inspectorate. One Inspectorate report on the quality of EMU joint work highlighted those factors which are seen to contribute to the success of any contact programme. Foremost of these is the active support of the head teacher and good working relationships between the head teachers of the linked schools. As far as class teachers are concerned, personal commitment to EMU and, again, good relationships between the teachers of the linked schools, are also essential for success. Careful planning and purposeful joint work mainly carried out in small groups are also important factors in ensuring the success of joint work. And success 'on the ground' is important in this whole area as in virtually no other. Joint work which fails can in fact damage relationships and can leave the situation worse than before. That is the high risk business in which all concerned are involved when they undertake EMU in Northern Ireland.

But is it all worth the effort? It is tempting to say that EMU in its various manifestations has been reasonably successful, and we are well on our way to some sort of Irish 'promised land'. But after so much murder, misunderstanding and mayhem our problems cannot be resolved quite as easily as that! The good effects of education are always slow to manifest themselves, and never more so than in a sensitive area like EMU. But if the progress is necessarily slow, I think there is at least some evidence to indicate that it is also steady. And even if it were not so, our only recourse would be to try again, for if education gives up on the young it has given up on the future and this would beg the whole question as to what education is really about. Some years ago a teacher with broad experience of promoting EMU in Northern Ireland brought the following extract to my attention. It has lived with me ever since: this letter was sent by the principal of an American high school to his staff.

Dear Teacher,
I am a survivor of a concentration
camp. My eyes saw what no man
should witness.

Gas chambers built by learned
engineers; children poisoned by
educated physicians; infants killed
by trained nurses; women and babies
shot and burned by high school and
college graduates.

So I am suspicious of Education.

My request is: help your students
become human. Your efforts must
never produce learned monsters,
skilled psychopaths, educated
Eichmanns.

We in education must try, and go on trying, to see to it that education makes what contribution it can to mutual understanding and tolerance for the sake of our young people, their future and ours.

I quoted from our poet Allingham at the beginning of my talk, and I will end with a quotation from another local poet John Hewitt (who comes from the Protestant tradition in Northern Ireland).

> *I walked that day with Willie Morrisey;*
> *While I still feared all priests he was my friend.*
> *Though clearly in the wrong, I would defend*
> *his right to his own dark mythology.*
> *You must give freedom if you would be free,*
> *for only friendship matters in the end.*[3]

John Hewitt is eloquent in describing how deep-seated his prejudices are, and how difficult they will be to erode. Dare I say that we would be less than honest if we were to pretend that all of us do not have equally strong prejudices, and, to be thoroughly realistic, so indeed it is with our teachers, and the children they teach. For we are all encumbered with a sizeable amount of baggage as we contemplate the challenge which EMU poses. In trying to explore what education can do to help, we must try to be equally clear in defining what it can not do. With this in mind, what lessons can we learn from our experience of including EMU in the Northern Ireland curriculum?

What did we get right? Where did we go wrong? What can education do, and not do? Might we have to be more modest than we would wish in our aspirations for EMU? Or, given the importance of the task, dare we let anything less than the sky be the limit? Whatever baggage he brings to his relationship with Willie Morrisey, John Hewitt concludes that 'only friendship matters in the end'. I confess that I would nearly settle for the outworking of that as one outcome of EMU. It is not miracles we can expect in our troubled land, but a return to old decencies between good neighbours and friends, and the right to entertain the thought that differences of opinion between them is the natural, normal way of the world – not to be feared; certainly to be tolerated; perhaps even to be celebrated!

NOTES

1. Lewis Carroll (Charles Lutwidge Dodgson), *Alice's Adventures in Wonderland* (Macmillan, 1901).
2. P.W. Joyce, *A Child's History of Ireland* (Longmans, Green, 1898), preface.
3. 'After the Fire' from *The Collected Poems of John Hewitt*, edited by Frank Ormsby (Blackstaff Press, 1991).

THE EUROPEAN STUDIES PROJECT: BROADENING HORIZONS

Elizabeth Armour

In 1988 the ministers of education of the member states of the European Community passed a resolution calling for an 'enhanced treatment of the European dimension in education as an element contributing to the development of the Community.' Today I am going to share with you experiences of my attempt to introduce and implement the whole idea of a European dimension within a secondary school in Northern Ireland.

Before joining the Inspectorate I spent 18 years teaching in a large boys' controlled secondary school in the north of Belfast. Pupil numbers were based around the 1,100 mark each year. The school was different to many others because although it was a secondary school it offered the full range of A levels, something that was generally reserved for the grammar schools of Northern Ireland. It had many other differences, not least the fact that it was situated in what was generally regarded as the most dangerous square mile in Northern Ireland. This particular area had witnessed more murders and other paramilitary activities than anywhere else in the province. The pupils attending the school had, for the most part, failed to secure a place at the local grammar school, but parents felt because of the reputation of the school that it could provide, for those who wanted it, the necessary requirements to go to university.

Most pupils came from loyalist, extreme loyalist or paramilitary backgrounds, where, even had they so desired, it would not have been deemed wise to associate with Roman Catholic pupils from across the community divide. Sadly, few opportunities existed for them to meet with, never mind take part in any meaningful activities with, other young people. Traditions, beliefs and cultural identities were passed down from one generation to another, and seldom did children differ in their views from those of their parents. For the many who did not go on to university, jobs existed in the area quite close to where they lived, so again it was a rare occasion when any meetings or encounters took place across the religious divide.

It was with great delight that we accepted a place in a project called the European Studies Project. This was aimed at pupils between the ages of 16 and 18 years, those who were generally in their first year of A level studies. Its aim was to enable pupils to study aspects of the development of Europe in the 20th century and to learn how the member states moved from the conflicts of two world wars to peaceful co-operation through organisations such as the European Union. The project had begun in the academic year 1986–87 with 12 schools from Northern Ireland, the Republic of Ireland, England and Belgium. These schools were hand-picked and in Northern Ireland were all from the grammar school sector. In the academic year 1987-88, the project 'hit reality'. By this I mean that they decided to take a chance on bringing on board a secondary school. It was relatively easy in the first year to ensure success, and avoid really extreme views, but was this the thrust that was needed? Were these pupils really going to benefit from the project? Surely they should move from the safety and security of the grammar schools into an inner-city school, with a great deal of political and paramilitary baggage? They did. We were in! But it was only years later that I discovered how many of them had feared the worst. Would someone be hurt – or worse – on the plane journey to Belgium? Would these tough Belfast lads really fit in? I think they did.

The project was organised and funded by the respective Departments of Education in both parts of Ireland, and it was a genuine attempt to familiarise these pupils with contemporary European issues and to provide a structure whereby they could initially look at their own views, face up to inhibiting factors in their own thinking, and acknowledge their fears of others' thinking, all within the framework of a European context. What did we do in this project? Obviously the whole idea of raising the pupils' awareness of the thinking and indeed the workings of what was then the European Community underpinned the whole programme. It must be remembered that at this time people in Northern Ireland were not greatly concerned with the workings of 'those people over in Europe' and felt that it did not affect them at all. The first thing which had to be done was to convince them that the European Community was here to stay and that it had advantages for young people. To ignore this would disable their thinking and reduce their opportunities in the future. This was not always easy. Many felt we had too many problems of our own. Why did they have to consider the problems of others? Some expressed the view that they did not work in Europe and would never want to. They did not even realise or acknowledge the fact that we were part of Europe. We battled haphazardly through the negatives, highlighting the need to be informed in order to compete in an ever-increasing European Community. We linked this with the promise of meeting girls from other European countries. This saved the day – they were interested!

We studied the main institutions of the Community, we considered the funding aspects, the role and importance of the European Parliament, and basically tried to figure out if there was any money in it for us. This was all very well, but did not do much for the pupils I referred to earlier. What advantage was it to know how the Structural Funds worked? Was this in any way going to help the pupils in their understanding of how other people thought, believed or reacted? What we had to do before attempting to understand the thinking of others was to clearly identify how we reacted to events, how we acknowledged the views of others, and most importantly how we could work alongside these others and gain or benefit from the extra understanding their experiences and personal views brought. It sounds quite straightforward, really. But how does one start?

As part of this programme, all schools had to identify local contemporary issues which they, the pupils, felt were worthy of consideration. One of the first issues we tackled was that of identifying our own cultural identity. I would always maintain that it was easier for my type of pupil to say what he or she was not, as opposed to explain what he or she believed in, aspired to or was in any way associated with. I was not to be proven wrong in this case. They quickly, but maybe not very clearly, established what they did not represent or believe in, but had great difficulty in establishing what they did believe in. How was I to overcome this problem? I did not and would not express my own views. We have heard already at this conference of some teachers' reluctance or reticence to come in and express their own personal identity. I still maintain that this is something which we should try to prevent happening – pupils should begin to think without any preconceived ideas from their teachers. So there was to be no teacher direction here. The pupils had to come up with what they truly felt. What hope had I of convincing them of the concept of a European identity, when they as yet had nothing to bring to it, or most likely felt they had nothing to gain from it?

The pupils could give no valid reasons for their aggressive thinking towards people holding different or opposing views to theirs. We researched the history books. We interviewed other people, teachers, parents, neighbours. Sadly, most, though with some exceptions, shared the views of the pupils. Was there no way out of this ever-increasing circle? We found that there was. We invited, for the first time, boys and girls from a Catholic grammar school to visit our school. This was not just to be a little cup of coffee and a pleasant chat. No – we were going to confront both groups, make them think, articulate their views, and express the views of others. We began by dividing them into mixed groups, setting tasks such as creating group identities, encompassing both beliefs and thinking, asking what Europe could do for them as young people, asking what Europe could do for Northern Ireland, and asking them what they felt Europe could do for them. We started to get some strand of common thinking, they began to realise that perhaps they had more in common than they had originally thought. A European election was imminent, so we set them the task of writing manifestos for various political parties, both those who opposed their thinking and those who represented their thinking. Finally we suggested a youth political party and they had to come up with their own strategies.

We did not always have agreement. We did not necessarily want agreement, but what we did have was a willingness to listen. That is not something people talking politics in Northern Ireland are particularly good at. The day ended with smiles. Nobody had changed their allegiances or beliefs – nobody had been asked to do so – but a start had been made. The communication lines were open. Contact had been begun. What happened then was dictated by the project – the introduction of communicating by electronic mail, not only with schools in Northern Ireland but also with schools in the Republic of Ireland, and England and Belgium as well. We wrote about our current issues. The pupils made a video which they sent to other schools. Part of this video involved some exciting role-play which saw them taking on the roles of people holding a different religion here in Northern Ireland. This was difficult – some had difficulty even saying the words, never mind including any expression or feeling!

Other issues included looking at sectarianism in the workplace, student grants, and the Troubles in general. I did not particularly want to look at this, but, to be fair, they had lived all their lives in a conflict which had an important bearing on their lives, so we tackled it. This later proved to be a great talking point when we visited Belgium in the summer. For the first two years of this project, eight pupils from each school were taken to Belgium to the Institute of European Affairs in Leuven. This was the highlight. Opportunities existed for a structured approach to discussion and debate. But I think the most beneficial outcomes were achieved in the informal setting of the evenings – probably they benefited much more without the teachers around!

This feature of the project existed for two years; but then the funding ceased. By now we felt it was too good to let go. News has cascaded down the school: in this corner of north Belfast, Europe was booming. Indeed, if you remember the time Britain pulled out of the Exchange Rate Mechanism and mortgage rates rose twice in one day, you can appreciate my concern when a parent rang me up pleading with me to do something. His son had mentioned that I was the woman in the school who dealt with Europe. What a responsibility to carry!

We could not let it go. Links had now been strengthened with a grammar school in Bandon in Cork. The difference between the two schools was striking, not least because of their rural background contrasting with my city slickers, but the social and economic trappings they possessed left my boys very much the poor relations. This did not matter. We visited them, and (with sincere thanks to their parents) they were allowed to visit and stay in Belfast. Yet again the bond and resilience of youth were coming through.

We maintained the project without the funds. We decided to fundraise and continue with the residentials either in Dublin or Belgium. This continued until last year, when I left the school. Numbers wishing to study Europe in the school increased. We widened the whole issue into the entire senior school, including those pupils who were studying for their General National Vocational Qualifications. We held our own 'Europe Days' which sometimes as many as 20 schools attended, including some from the Republic of Ireland. We celebrated 'Europe Day' each year in the school, with a high number of staff and departments joining in. We held 'Beauty Evenings for the young European Woman' to raise money – quite a feat in a boys' school! We visited and debated in the European Parliament. We held a conference taking Europe into the 21st century, again with many other schools participating. And all this despite the fact that there was no funding available!

What did the pupils get out of this whole thing? Understanding, clarity of thinking about their own views, the ability to articulate their own viewpoints, a knowledge of where they stand or what they represent in the world of politics, an ability to make sense of the idea of the European Union, an acceptance that others do not always share their views, a tolerance of those other views and an ability to accept that other views are valid and not always threatening. Friendships, not least with people they would not normally have met, have kept going over the years. Visits to Cork take place every year and many former pupils go back to visit Leuven, sometimes taking their parents with them. Many talk about that year being the changing point in their lives. While I would not presume to have had so much influence over their lives, it pleased me to think that I at least presented them with opportunities to look further and indeed to broaden their horizons.

The project still exists, though in a slightly modified fashion. At present there are 352 schools participating, which is very rewarding when we remember it began with only 12 schools. Thank you for giving me the opportunity to share these views with you, and I hope you learned something about the thinking of the young men from North Belfast.

TEACHING CONTROVERSIAL ISSUES

Peter D. Logue

I would like to add my welcome to the overseas visitors and thank the organisers of the conference for the opportunity to say something about the role of television in addressing controversial issues. I would like to begin by considering the Lambeg drum. This was originally a European war drum, and it is fantastically resonant – if you have ever been close to one at a parade or a drumming competition, you will never forget it! And this brings to mind one of Seamus Heaney's early poems, in which he describes marchers coming home from a Twelfth of July parade, near his south Derry village of Bellaghy, tired yet exhilarated. Heaney's description of the drum-carrier is one of the most tantalising, even agonising paradoxes I have ever encountered, and I think, especially in my darker moments, that it is a good metaphor for this society: 'Buoyed up by what he buckles under'. It may be controversial to suggest it, but I think sometimes we in this society, unionist and nationalist, are buoyed up by this conflict just as much as we buckle under it. Do we have a psychosis so that we need this conflict? Even at a time when Europe is beginning to come together, we still have these nightmares, these disintegrations, these bitternesses, these separations. Sometimes I think about our education system and wish that in schooling there could be more buoying up than buckling under. I would say that the reason I am involved in this type of education for mutual understanding of work is because I do not think there is any alternative, even if our successes are hugely qualified.

Channel 4 (the 'channel with attitude') was set up under the Broadcasting Act 1981 and was put in business to cater for tastes, interests and audiences not touched by other UK broadcasters. During the 15 years of its existence it has pursued a vigorous policy of multiethnic, multicultural, pluralist programming. It has also had more than its fair share of controversy, producing dramas involving murder and incest as almost daily fare, political exposés such as the 'Arms to Iraq' scandal and alleged collusion between Loyalist para-

69

militaries and the RUC. It has also broadcast many late-night ruderies
– in short, there has been no shortage on Channel 4 of programmes
which provoke people to complain. But there is a strong consensus
within this country, supported by some opinion from abroad, that
whatever its perceived faults, Channel 4 has been a major source of
innovation, energy and creativity. It has also made a phenomenal contribution to the development of the contemporary British film industry and been responsible for a major growth in the independent
production sector in this country.

In 1990 David Mellor introduced a new Broadcasting Act which
effectively changed the whole broadcasting landscape in the UK.
Channel 4 was repositioned as a commercial channel required to sell
advertising airtime for its own survival. The channel's original remit
for multicultural and minority interests remained, but week in, week
out, the controllers are faced with a daily balancing act between commercial survival and the provision of a strong, culturally responsible
public service. They have not made too bad a job of it.

In keeping with what schools have been doing for generations, in
this place and elsewhere in the UK and in Ireland, Channel 4, the
BBC and ITV have been making schools programmes for nearly 35
years, which have looked at and promoted an appreciation of
European cultural diversity. We have made programmes on history,
geography, music, art and languages, including the lesser-spoken
languages. So there are thousands of hours of output which have
been of help to teachers in all sorts of subjects.

The title of this session, which refers to the teaching of controversial issues, is a bit of a misnomer, because it is far more about using
television, in an attempt to help young people unravel difficulties
which can make everyday life sometimes painful and awkward. I do
not think that television, even educational television, is particularly
good at the straightforward didactic method – it is much more of an
impressionistic and suggestive medium. This work, of which we have
heard so much which has been fascinating over the past couple of
days, if it is to be successful at all, has got to attach as much importance to the context, process, and ethos of the whole situation as it
must to the context. Television as a resource is only a part of that. And
I would like to point out here two things which separate mainstream
television from programmes for schools: first, schools' television programmes are designed to be mediated in specific contexts by teachers, and are designed and fashioned in close consultation with
teachers, curriculum specialists and with pupils as well, in many

instances. They have to be, in a schooling system where curriculum content is very seriously prescribed, otherwise people would not use them. And, second, these programmes are not an end in themselves. Rather, they require a process which is ongoing with other activities; they presume that there is going to be speaking and listening, reading and writing, looking for evidence, carrying out experiments and so forth, so it is never presumed that they are a narrative process which young people watch from start to finish. We assume that teachers are going to be editors who pick and choose and encourage the schoolchildren to do the same. And I would also point out to our overseas visitors that there is a well-established infrastructure in the UK which involves the BBC and Channel 4 sending out, each Easter, annual catalogues of over 300 hours of programmes which are going to be broadcast in the coming academic year. This allows teachers to plan their resources very carefully.

Channel 4 has produced a unit of some fascinating programmes, which teachers have told us have been very successful, on issues like drugs, sex, violence, racism and other controversial issues such as blood sports, vegetarianism, the future of the monarchy, euthanasia – there is no shortage of issues on which to make programmes. The traditional locus for much of this work in Channel 4's output is a strand called 'Personal, Social and Health Education', and you will find many of the programmes just referred to in our own upper secondary school strand of films called 'Off Limits'. But one thing we are not sure about is how teachers can use very powerful drama. The narrative experience of this on its own is often sufficient. As an example I would mention an especially powerful drama (which was given in a fine production by Replay here in Belfast a short time ago) from a Dutch playwright, Ad de Bont, called 'Mirad, a Boy from Bosnia'. This deals with the situation in Bosnia-Herzegovina and Croatia. It is told in flashback and begins on Mirad's 13th birthday, which was the day before the declaration of the independence of Bosnia on 8 April 1992. Soon afterwards, Mirad's village is invaded by the Serbs. His sister is killed by mortar shrapnel and dies in his arms, his mother disappears, and his father, along with a dozen other men, is made to walk through a minefield in front of the boy who sees him blown to pieces. Mirad crosses the minefield without regard to his own safety and buries his father's dismembered hand. He makes his way to Sarajevo to his uncle and aunt but is again imprisoned. However, he is released and eventually sent to Holland with the help of the Red Cross.

One of the most significant features of television in teaching controversial issues is that it provides an essential third-party point of reference – we all know about the difficulties of working in an area where there is such emotion and often such pain that issues about disclosure, or security for young people, are very important; hence the significance of a parallel experience such as this (and we can recognise some of the dangers inherent in that nightmare that are incipient in this society). So I have no doubt that in the hands of skilled mediators, a drama like that can be used to enormously good effect. At the heart of the play is the anguished cry of the displaced refugee, but more terrifying for us is the uncompromising representation of what happens when ethnic prejudices, bigotries and fears are allowed to harden into political expression and are manipulated by cynical politicians.

Finally, there is a series called 'Off The Walls' which has its origins in a decision taken by Channel 4 in 1993, at the time of two notorious atrocities in Northern Ireland, at Greysteel and on the Shankill. We took a decision that we were going to make a significant input into the work of EMU, in order to try to promote greater understanding, looking at aspects of identity in Northern Ireland. In a sense we got lucky because the ceasefire was declared shortly after we made this decision. The series consists of five 20-minute programmes which in a sense reflect the optimism of that early period. It draws on a mix of drama (one is about a range of stereotypical young people from different backgrounds), documentary (filmed essays from Jerusalem looking at the experiences of Jewish and Arab young people), studio debate (between young people from Northern Ireland), and also some animated sequences (especially one dealing with poet John Hewitt's image of a flags-and-emblems knot tangling and disentangling). This mix is able to present a sort of distancing perspective which we think in some senses helps in the films. As someone who worked for many years in educational broadcasting for adults, I think broadcasting is at its best when it is actually catalysing creative partnerships among educational providers and others in the community. We in Channel 4 are enormously indebted to a whole range of key groups, to the Department of Education, the University of Ulster, the Education and Library Boards and all other parties who helped to produce this project. Marian O'Doherty will tell you shortly some more about how the films are used.

In some senses this is a development model, and we could possibly have made some better films if we had the experimental work with teachers ahead of the production process. I would also like to point out that we got some European Union funding from its PSEP Teacher Training Programme, which encourages teachers from different disciplines to work together looking for appropriate methodologies with which to use these films. And it was the support of Ulster Television and Channel 4 which really kick-started the grant-making process.

I will now invite Marian to talk about the project in some depth.

THE 'SPEAK YOUR PIECE' PROJECT

Marian O'Doherty

I want now to give you some insight into the two-year 'Speak Your Piece' project, which has been trying to address some of the controversial issues that concern young people, and indeed all of us, in Northern Ireland. 'Off The Walls', the Channel 4 series, is our main resource. We have also produced a booklet, 'Exploring Controversial Issues', to complement the programme and to help teachers and others to work through the issues with young people. The project itself has brought together teachers from 20 schools and youth workers from 21 youth organisations. These groupings are themselves often perceived as coming from very different cultures, and although we are all working with young people, there is for that reason not necessarily a lot of contact. Moreover, the young person's day is divided between school, and the very different youth club in the evening. The teachers and the youth workers have come together with us in the project, using the 'Off The Walls' series and booklet to explore five themes with young people: identity, culture, religion, politics, and future choices. These are explored and debated among young people, and the work of the project is underpinned by three guiding principles:

- enabling dialogue which is forthright and inclusive – extremely difficult in Northern Ireland for those facilitating as well as those participating in discussion;
- providing alternatives to violence and avoidance of the issues as a means of responding to conflict;
- facilitating participatory decision-making which encourages democratic processes.

It is all very well to have these on paper, but it is the practice of them which is the important, but also the difficult part. We have therefore tried to involve ourselves in a process with young people, a process about promoting core values of freedom and democracy, and of equality, and by encouraging practitioners to use activities which encourage an open sharing of all our biographies. We have all been touched by what we have seen and heard, whether from friends, from family or from community. We want to try to inform young people of a range of alternative views and opinions, using the media and our own experiences, and guest speakers. We also want to show them that there are multiple perspectives on any issue. They have a right to their view, but others have that right as well. We want to clarify and resolve any internal conflicts they may have. We want to give them opportunities where not only can they express their kind of idea of what our society should be about, but where they are also open to see that on wider issues and in a wider debate there might be fair outcomes and fairer outcomes according to what position you hold in society or what position you have taken within a society. Finally, and perhaps most importantly, we want young people to be involved in a process which encourages creative thinking in responding to controversial issues. One of the controversies at the moment is on marching and one young person during an inclusive dialogue suggested that we march just every other year. That might not be the best solution but we must admit it is creative in one way! We want opportunities for young people to say those sorts of things and to negotiate and challenge each other.

We have discovered that much of the fear and concern which surrounds this type of work is that the work itself can lead to conflict. We have to resolve that problem as well including teachers and young people in a training dimension, because there is very often a conflict between our own core and cherished values which have been passed on to us through our families, our churches and our communities, and which we aspire to and hope to pass on to a younger generation. But in educational terms, what we are trying to do is to help young people and indeed ourselves to unpack and unravel and unbind our own consciousness of what our culture is and the many, many ways in which we inherit it; not to free ourselves of cultural traditions, which is one of the concerns of the people who sit very much outside this work, but really to learn to understand our traditions and, more importantly to learn how to articulate them in non-violent ways.

A further problem, which has caused a lot of concern and depression for teachers and others involved in this work, is: how can we find solutions when society is still grappling with the problem? What we are trying to do as a project is not to take a step forward but to ask people to take a step back with us so that we can help young people to have the skills to engage in a complex discourse, not necessarily to find solutions but to actually become involved in the educational process of that complexity. And also to gradually bring them to realise and to intellectualise the complications, the diversities, the values and the conflicts of our cultural identities.

EUROPEAN PROGRAMMES IN THE FIELD
OF EDUCATION

Cesare Onestini

The European Union, through the European Commission, has set up a number of projects and programmes for co-operation in education. The level of participation by schools in Northern Ireland is disappointingly small, and in some programmes there is none at all. One reason for this is that the existence of these programmes is not as well known as it should be. What then are the benefits of these programmes? There are lessons to be learned from co-operation with other schools across Europe, a basic idea similar to the EMU programme in Northern Ireland schools, although the issues dealt with would not be exactly the same.

A look at these co-operation projects shows that what guides them is the idea of cultural diversity, which is what Europe is about – it is in its nature, and unavoidable. And this does not just mean cultural diversity in terms of different existing nationalities, but also involves these nationalities mixing together, which is one of the aims of the European Union. It is now the norm in schools across Europe to have children from many different cultural backgrounds, speaking numerous languages: statistics show that this trend is growing. I am sure that such a trend would also be visible in Northern Ireland. Any education system, today, will have to take into account this growing cultural diversity, not least because, more and more, going into employment will involve mobility and some sort of encounter with different cultures and languages. Schools should plan for this.

I shall now to set out the European projects in the field of education. The Treaty of Maastricht, Article 126, states:

The Community shall contribute to the development of quality education by encouraging co-operation between Member States and, if necessary, by supporting and supplementing their action, while fully respecting the responsibility of the Member States for

the content of teaching and the organisation of educational systems and their cultural and linguistic diversity.

This shows that, while education is basically a national issue, it has
now been recognised, by this recent Treaty, that there is scope for
action at the European level: the EU has a role in promoting action.
Its programmes in the field of education now embrace 18 countries –
outside the EU, Norway, Iceland and Liechtenstein are already
involved, and other countries may soon join, from central Europe or
the eastern Mediterranean.

There are three main programmes in the field of education: the
Socrates programme, the Leonardo Da Vinci programme and the
Youth for Europe programme. These are, respectively, for the pro-
motion of co-operation in the fields of education, professional and
vocational training, and youth activities. All are run by the
Directorate-General for Education, Training and Youth (Directorate-
General No XXII).

I shall concentrate on the Socrates programme, and in particular
that part dealing with schools, Comenius. Socrates is divided into
three parts or chapters. The first is Erasmus, which is the best-known
and longest-running. It began ten years ago, and relates to universities and students. The second chapter is Comenius, which began in
1995 and involves all activities dealing with co-operation between
schools across Europe. Finally there is a chapter involving what are
known as 'horizontal' measures – these concern such matters as the
improvement of languages, open and distance learning, or adult education.

Comenius is itself divided into three activities or 'actions', each
having slightly different target groups and aims. Action 1, the most
important in terms of numbers and budget, involves partnerships
between schools, whereby schools from different member states work
on a joint European Education Project. There are now about 2,300 of
these in operation, each having at least three schools involved.

Action 2 involves Transnational Projects which address, first, the
educational needs of the children of migrant workers, occupational
travellers, travellers and gypsies; and second, intercultural education
for all pupils. The second element (intercultural education of all
pupils), addresses the issue of curriculum development and mutual
understanding, and projects under this theme can be strikingly similar to some of the EMU projects in Northern Ireland. I shall now go
through some of the essential points relating to this action.

The Comenius school partnerships, as I have said, function in a similar way to the Northern Ireland EMU programmes. The aim is simply to introduce and promote the European dimension in schools. Some money is given to each participating school. The essential point is that there must be a well-identified aim, there must be support from teachers and headteachers, and there must be a clear timetable. The existing projects, all of which are quite new, are currently being promoted with a lot of energy, and funding is not in short supply. In the four largest countries (Germany, the United Kingdom, France and Italy), not all of the allocated funds have been taken up, for the simple reason that in bigger countries, there is less geographical proximity between schools as compared with, say, Belgium or the Netherlands. The trend at the moment is such that more of these projects will be initiated, and everything is done to help schools take part.

A project will typically have a multidisciplinary approach, seeking to embrace all school activities. Also encouraged are teacher mobility, the use of new technology, and contact with neighbouring schools not themselves partners in the project.

Action 2 of Comenius is more specifically targeted. I should like particularly to explain a little about intercultural education. The support given to cultural education projects varies according to the nature of the proposals received. The guidelines used are very open, in terms of who can apply – whether schools, associations, local authorities, non-governmental organisations, the only essential is that the project be transnational with participants from at least three countries. We have many different kinds of project. Some focus on the curriculum – for example, how to teach geography in an intercultural setting: which curricular and teaching methodologies do you need? Some projects are more action-oriented – for example, the role of language in primary schools: how should teachers approach a class comprised of pupils coming from mixed cultures, having different abilities, and coming from a wide variety of socioeconomic backgrounds? Other projects explore the inter-faith dialogue, or inner-city schools – there is no limit to the range of the 150 or so projects currently in operation. The only requirement is that the participants joining together to create them must come from different cultures.

How then does the European Commission help? Comenius Action 2 gives financial support to transnational projects with the participation of at least three countries and two organisations per country. It encourages different types of organisation working together. The financial support consists of grants, awarded for one year but renewable for another two. These grants will vary according to the nature of the activities, but will usually be at a level of 50 per cent of the total costs. Awards may also be given (up to 1,000 ecus) for preparatory visits.

Comenius Action 3 involves projects for in-service training of teachers and others involved in education The importance of such teacher training courses cannot be overestimated. Nothing can be done without teacher participation, and Action 3 exists to acknowledge this. The European Commission can assist in the preparation of training packs, creating courses, making videos, and so on; it can also provide travel grants for individuals to travel anywhere in Europe to take part in one of these courses.

The European Union began these projects in 1995. They represent a new kind and level of co-operation. I would encourage you to consider them not just for your own interest but also as a means of further promoting European co-operation in your region and in your schools.

THE IMPACT OF EDUCATION FOR MUTUAL UNDERSTANDING

Alan Smith

During the past 25 years of the conflict in Northern Ireland several educational strategies have emerged partly in response to the conflict itself and partly in response to the fact that a majority of our children attend segregated schools. Of these, three main strategies have come to prominence.

First, since the early 1970s there have been a number of pro-grammes, some carried out through formal education and others through less formal approaches, of what some people call 'cross-com-munity contact' programmes. These involve Catholic and Protestant young people being given the opportunity to work or socialise together in some joint endeavour. These programmes have increased in number over the years, and finally received government support in 1987 through a scheme whereby schools and youth groups have access to a budget of some £1,000,000 per year. Recent research shows that 40 per cent of primary schools and 60 per cent of sec-ondary schools take part in programmes of this kind, although only 10 per cent of all their pupils are actually involved. There are mixed reactions to the various programmes and accusations of social engi-neering or of being merely cosmetic. It is the quality of what has hap-pened in the programmes which is really being questioned when these issues are raised.

A second initiative, from the early 1980s, is known as 'planned inte-grated schooling'. The first such school opened in 1981 – today there are 32 of them. In these schools, Protestant and Catholic children are educated together in roughly equal numbers. There are in total about 7,000 pupils at these schools; this represents only 3 per cent of all schoolchildren in Northern Ireland. The majority of schoolchild-ren – about one-third of a million in all – continue to attend either Catholic schools or schools which are predominantly Protestant in their enrolment.

Partly in an attempt to address the needs of these children, there has been a third initiative, the development of curriculum programmes which study issues related to identity and conflict, and cultural diversity in Northern Ireland. Of these programmes, probably the best known is 'Education for Mutual Understanding' or EMU. Associated with it is a complementary theme known as 'Cultural Heritage'. Although their roots are in the early 1970s, it was not until the late 1980s that the government backed these more explicitly – in 1989 they became a mandatory, statutory feature of the curriculum for all schools in Northern Ireland.

EMU is not a subject as such but a cross-curricular theme having four very abstract and broad objectives. These are to enable pupils:

- to respect and value themselves and others;
- to begin to appreciate the interdependence of people within our society and further afield;
- to explore something of their own and other cultural traditions;
- to gain some practical experience of how to understand and cope with conflict, whether in their personal, social or political lives.

These are fairly grand ideals; my particular interest in the past five years has been in how these themes were introduced into the statutory curriculum, and I would like to comment on the messages we have received from teachers, pupils and youth workers in our education system about the effectiveness and impact of this kind of approach.

There are some positive things we can point to right away. Although the cross-community contact is not a compulsory feature of the programmes, it is very often associated with the EMU programmes and there has been a change in climate compared to ten years ago: there is now a far higher level of contact between Protestant and Catholic schoolchildren. I am constantly reminded by my elders and betters, when I get frustrated at the pace at which the programmes are having some impact, that in their own time there was far more rigid separation and much less capacity for interaction between young people from the two religious backgrounds. EMU has created a climate of opportunity for educators, whether working in formal or informal situations, to move away from the old environment.

Another positive thing is that while previously teachers were always looking over their shoulders to see what parents, the school management or people in the wider community thought about this kind of work, the introduction of EMU has really brought parental support for it a bit more into the open. I was involved a few years ago in researching how much support there was among parents for these kinds of programmes, and teachers were often surprised at the level of inter-school contact which parents were hoping they would create: 25 per cent of parents felt this should be happening on a daily basis and thereby seemed to be reflecting on their own disappointment at not having been able, at school age, to satisfy their curiosity about the peers separated from them by the formal structures of the education system. This is heartening, and I will I hope be an encouragement to teachers to take advantage of the opportunities now provided.

A further positive feature is a whole new language, not just in the education system but in society more generally, a language about mutual respect and tolerance, parity of esteem, equal respect for different cultural traditions, and so on. We have seen, in the formal education system and also in the more informal youth activities, that this language is becoming the legitimate public vocabulary, and though we might be cynical about how our politicians use it, it is a language which was not visible just a few years ago.

From my own academic point of view, the most encouraging sign is that whereas only five years ago, to make any critical comment about these programmes would make people seem either unsupportive of them, or somehow politically incorrect, that climate has changed, and it is possible to ask more critical questions about the effectiveness of the programmes themselves. This is done in the spirit of not trying to throw the baby out with the bathwater in the sense that young people's aspirations and parents' expectations are that education has a very positive role in trying to provide opportunities for our young people to engage with some of the more difficult, sensitive and politically divisive issues in our society. So we have moved a long way from the position that schools should be insulated from issues in society around us, pretending they do not exist.

In terms of criticism, there are four areas of difficulty experienced by teachers. The first is: what exactly are the key issues to grapple with and to engage our young people? We have tried to listen to what teachers identify as the issues which, as a society, we should be presenting to our young people. They aren't all particular to Northern Ireland, but one which goes to the heart of the problem in Northern Ireland is the issue of identity – who we are, how we express ourselves in terms of our language, culture, religion, and politics. Teachers told us that the exploration of identity should be a key activity in which to engage our young people. There are more specific issues, such as the understanding of the contemporary history of Northern Ireland. The recent curriculum review tried to establish where young people learn about this – is it a compulsory feature or merely an option in the curriculum? I recall one British politician saying that history stopped ten years ago; after that it is politics, and thus too controversial to deal with.

A second issue relevant to this conference is the role of the media. How can we get our young people to develop a critical faculty for reading the messages which interpret events around them? This is seen as another important area. Other areas include the administration of justice, the law, and civic education. Unlike some European countries, Northern Ireland has no clearly focused area in the school curriculum which forms for all young people a civic or political education. There is also the issue of equality of opportunity, especially as the persistent 'two traditions' view ensures that issues of equality of opportunity permeate right throughout society in Northern Ireland. Politics and decision-making, democracy in our society – how can our young people be brought to feel that they have a say in these areas in our society? And we cannot forget the issues of violence and sectarianism, and attitudes to these.

This is a formidable list which is a considerable challenge to educators. Implicit in drawing up this list is a recognition that we are not actually addressing the issues in the best way possible. But if we have a clear idea of which issues to address, how do we fit them into our curriculum? There are basically three ways in which this can be done.

The first is infusion of the curriculum, that is, to encourage a root-and-branch review of all our areas of study and to try to integrate this whole agenda of issues through every subject across the curriculum. The benefit of this would be that teachers, already committed personally to their subjects, would handle the agenda in a committed and thoughtful way. But in reality, some subjects are more amenable to this infusion than others. We have found that the teachers who tend to get heavily involved in such work teach subjects like history, religion and English.

A second strategy would be to permeate the curriculum – that is, not asking every teacher to take on the whole agenda, but to ask teachers in a more collective sense to share the load, so that some aspects of this agenda may be carried through particular subjects but co-ordinated with what is happening in other subjects. This is basically the approach used at the moment. But it does have weaknesses. There is a real danger that the necessary co-ordination for an effective strategy does not exist at school level. Or, the work may be ghettoised so that one particularly enthusiastic teacher will end up carrying the whole agenda for the whole school.

A third option would be a dedicated space within the curriculum in which to grapple with the more complicated issues. We do not have this at the moment and achieving it is probably quite difficult given the current demands on the core curriculum. But, looking at our immediate neighbours, there is a debate going on in Britain, probably reacting to the perceived moral decline in society, as to whether we should have a dedicated time given to the issue of citizenship, or social and moral education. In the Republic of Ireland, a pilot programme at secondary school called 'Civic, Social and Political Education' replaced a more out-dated formal civics programme which operated for one period per week as part of the formal entitlement for all pupils.

There are also questions as to which is the most important strategy. My own claim is that we should ideally try to be inclusive. There is an opportunity between now and the next formal review of the curriculum, in the year 2001, to begin to grapple not only with determining the issues but devising the best strategies for trying to embed this work in a meaningful way within the curriculum.

A third criticism of EMU is the extent to which schools are taking it seriously. There was considerable debate, at the time it was introduced to the curriculum, about whether making something statutory and compulsory is the best way – is coercion a useful strategy? Some schools have taken what we term a minimalist approach to EMU – in other words, they look at what they are required to do by law, basically to reassure themselves that they are covering the broad objectives through each subject in the curriculum. Such an approach does not really follow the spirit of what the theme is about. So there are minus points to coercion. On the other hand, it does give a foothold for this kind of work in a curriculum which is becoming increasingly technocratic and knowledge and content-based. A movement beyond the minimalist approach needs a degree of vision within the senior management of schools which creates a climate in which teachers feel safe, supported and able to tackle what are, after all, not very easy issues. So perhaps more energy should be concentrated on senior staff in order to create a more holistic vision of the climate and relationships within the schools, relationships between a school and the community it serves, and the extent to which the school is itself a democratic institution.

Finally, but also most importantly, if there was a single message coming from teachers, it was that they too had considerable reservations about their own capacity to engage with the new agenda I have been describing. In part that may have been because their initial training had not provided the opportunity to develop the skills or to become familiar with the issues which are now pressing. But it is also to do with the training they received for a different reason – that it did not really address all of the emotional and value-related areas which are part and parcel of getting involved in this sort of work. Teachers regretted the fact that they had had very little opportunity to reflect on these issues, which throw up very strong emotions within society. Everyone has their own tradition, culture and background and it is very difficult not to bring these into the teaching arena. So the type of training is probably as important as the issues it deals with.

That, I suppose, leaves us with the challenge, of developing the whole agenda to tackle these problems, of taking EMU seriously, of trying to address some of the more difficult issues. We need to work on a wide range of fronts. There is a new curriculum for the youth organisations within which are opportunities for political education and values in society to be addressed explicitly by youth workers. As we work towards the Curriculum Review in 2001 we should either infuse or permeate the curriculum at all levels with practical approaches supporting the aims and objectives of EMU, or develop a human rights agenda which might move Northern Ireland from the parochial to the universal. That is a considerable challenge, but would equip our teachers with understanding of the basic values and principles underpinning human rights which are valued in our society and beyond and would also address any reservation about an internal liberal agenda.

There are four years to effect a transformation, to try to move, if not our whole curriculum, then certainly many aspects of it and particularly EMU, onto the firmer basis of the principles of human rights. If this could be achieved it would be fine, but only half the job, because the curriculum is only as strong as the people who deliver it, and we cannot neglect those aspects of training and professional development which encourage our teachers to develop the capacity to deal with complex issues effectively, confidently, and in a secure environment. That means looking at the whole range of educational provisions, whether at initial level, at the induction phase for those teachers newly arrived in the profession, or at the further professional development level. It is as much to do with the type of training required as with the practice in schools and youth organisations. This means working at developing new resources and effective methodologies, looking at all sorts of information and educational technologies and their ability to contribute to this area of work. Hopefully we are making some steps in these directions.

Not everything in the garden is always rosy. There is always a temptation, especially with overseas visitors as at this conference, to present ourselves in the best light. I think we can say with a certain pride that we are trying to engage with the issues. But there is no room for complacency and it would be foolish to think that we did not have a long way to go in terms of developing more effective approaches.

THE CONTRIBUTION OF THE ARTS, LANGUAGE AND MUSEUMS TO CULTURAL DIVERSITY

THE ROLE OF THE ARTS COUNCIL IN CULTURAL POLICY

Donnell Deeny

The Arts Council is the servant of art. Art is the highest expression of cultural traditions; it is rooted in them, but not bounded by them – this gives art both its validity and its power to communicate at the deepest level with its community, and also its salvation – its ability to transcend the borders of language, local detail and nationality.

The Arts Council is the older colleague of those organisations dedicated to community relations and the fostering of a better understanding of cultural traditions in Northern Ireland, many of which are represented at this conference. What distinguishes it from other cultural organisations though, is that the Council has no brief to modify or temper artistic expression; this is no part of its remit, even as an ambition. But this is no licence for propaganda. Art transforms ideas and aspirations which already exist. The fact has been well understood by the outgoing Minister of Education in his enlightened agreement to enshrine, in the Arts Council (Northern Ireland) Order 1995, an 'arm's length' policy with regard to the Council's artistic judgement.

It may therefore be misleading to speak of the role of the Arts Council in 'cultural policy' as that might imply something that does not in fact exist. Policy relates to how we support and encourage the arts but not to what the culture of our citizens ought to be.

In the last revenue allocations, the Arts Council disbursed over £6.5 million to more than 200 arts organisations in Northern Ireland. In addition, the Council supports the artistic achievement of close to 1,000 individual artists in all fields of the arts. With knock-on multiplier effects, as John Myerscough points out, the arts as a whole contribute between 8,300 and 9,000 jobs to the economy; the Arts Council sustains around 1,600 of those directly as full-time posts.[1]

Also, the Council has since May 1995 allocated £12.5 million from the National Lottery Arts Fund to 236 arts organisations. Through the Lottery, the Council has been able to enhance radically the

91

opportunities for both conventional arts organisation and new arts initiatives taken at a local community level to amplify arts provision right across Northern Ireland. This is no small achievement, but it is one in which at the moment we are in the period between word and deed. The Lottery has added to the steady flowering of the distinctive arts of Northern Ireland over the last 40 years an extraordinary and new energy which, when the new theatres and arts centres open in the near future, will constitute a startling leap forward, or in the words (in another context) of Seamus Heaney, 'a lure let down to tempt the soul to rise'.

It has been the arts in Northern Ireland which have been in the forefront of vying with violence for international coverage. Whatever about the short-term impact of violent acts on the minds of those who watch television or read newspapers abroad or at home, it is our arts which extend the longest-lasting effect. Our painters, our dramatists, our novelists, our musicians, our actors and, of course, our poets have raised a creative consciousness of Northern Ireland abroad which will prove resistant to the explosive impact of negative images, in the long term, which is always where the arts come into their own.

These artists are of quite exceptional distinction for a population of only a million and a half. The poets Seamus Heaney, Louis MacNeice, John Montague, Derek Mahon, Paul Muldoon, Ciaran Carson (the latter two both TS Eliot Prize winners); the pianist Barry Douglas, and the flautist James Galway; the playwright Brian Friel; the novelist Brian Moore; the actors Liam Neeson, Stephen Rea and Kenneth Branagh have all won renown beyond these shores. They also have many distinguished peers.

It can be seen from this that most of our work, and that of artists, is not dictated to by the Troubles but seeks to provide a full range of arts to our citizens in the way that any similar agency in continental Europe would do. We sustain the high arts, as they are sometimes called, but also reach out our hand to encourage new participation by those to whom the arts seem alien.

The arts generally can make an enormous contribution to our society at this time of hope and change. They can play a vigorous part in the process of reconciliation, in providing employment and improving the quality of life for both our own people and those coming to the province for business and pleasure.

The Arts Council maintains a responsibility to the long-term future of the imagination in Northern Ireland; often, that responsibility is exercised quietly in the day-to-day security of arts organisations which

FAST FOTO <No.26 >027
537 20** N N N N-22 (046)©

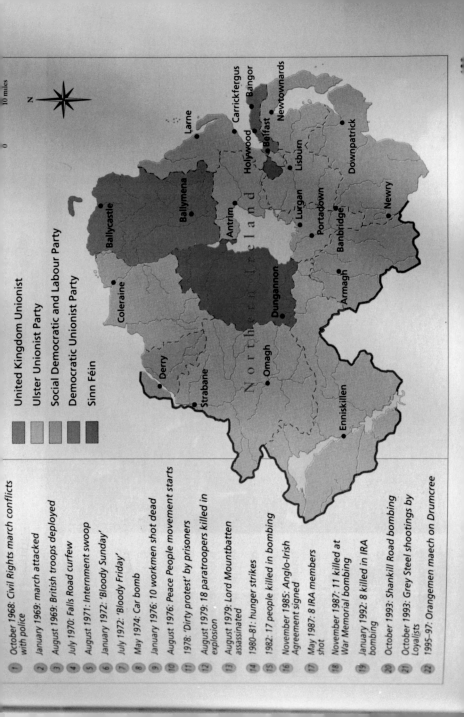

Legend (political parties):
- United Kingdom Unionist
- Ulster Unionist Party
- Social Democratic and Labour Party
- Democratic Unionist Party
- Sinn Féin

Timeline events:

1. October 1968: Civil Rights march conflicts with police
2. January 1969: march attacked
3. August 1969: British troops deployed
4. July 1970: Falls Road curfew
5. August 1971: Internment swoop
6. January 1972: 'Bloody Sunday'
7. July 1972: 'Bloody Friday'
8. May 1974: Car bomb
9. January 1976: 10 workmen shot dead
10. August 1976: Peace People movement starts
11. 1978: 'Dirty protest' by prisoners
12. August 1979: 18 paratroopers killed in explosion
13. August 1979: Lord Mountbatten assassinated
14. 1980–81: hunger strikes
15. 1982: 17 people killed in bombing
16. November 1985: Anglo-Irish Agreement signed
17. May 1987: 8 IRA members shot
18. November 1987: 11 killed at War Memorial bombing
19. January 1992: 8 killed in IRA bombing
20. October 1993: Shankill Road bombing
21. October 1993: Grey Steel shootings by Loyalists
22. 1995–97: Orangemen maech on Drumcree

Map labels:
Larne, Carrickfergus, Bangor, Newtownards, Belfast, Holywood, Lisburn, Downpatrick, Ballycastle, Ballymena, Antrim, Lurgan, Portadown, Banbridge, Newry, Coleraine, Dungannon, Armagh, Derry, Omagh, Strabane, Enniskillen

Northern Ireland

0   10 miles

N

are modestly funded, but with far from modest ambitions. I think of a simple grant made by the Council to a community arts group in Greysteel, County Londonderry. In 1993, that small town had been the focus of the world's attention because of an horrific massacre which took place there one week after an equally horrific and murderous bomb blast on the Shankill Road in Belfast. Almost two years later, when the headlines had disappeared and the world had long since turned its attention elsewhere, the Arts Council was able, through the Artist in the Community scheme, to assist a cross-community group to fashion out of its experiences a quiet, durable, genuinely artistic achievement.

Part of the Council's role is to protect the artist from the philistine. Sometimes, these philistines masquerade as something else. A prominent politician had called for Arts Council support for what he described as 'British Art'. He turned out not to be referring to Damien Hirst or the Brit Pack but, after some evasions, to pipe bands – which the Council has supported and continues to support.

I am inclined to think, however, that he had in mind a suspicion of art from the continent of Europe which would be commonly heard in every British city. Handel and Haydn, Mozart and Beethoven – foreign, and therefore dubious. This confused suspicion of the arts is, I believe, diminishing. 'High' and 'popular' art have always mixed, but do so even more now.

Another area of controversy has been that of arts in the Irish language. Some seem to resent any spending in this area, even though Irish music, dancing and poetry in particular have a proud and vibrant tradition. Others, for example some republican politicians who claim to support such arts, complain that we spend too little in that area. But their advocacy is inevitably weakened by their simultaneous support for violence and terrorism. We may not remember whether Handel, Haydn, Mozart and Beethoven were Catholic or Protestant but we can be sure they never sat on any kangaroo court or used iron bars or hurley sticks to break the legs and arms of their fellow citizens in so-called 'punishment' beatings.

The arts may celebrate disorder at times but, perhaps paradoxically, they require order in which to blossom. What art came out of the dark ages of Europe in the first millennium? Answer: the Book of Kells and the Book of Armagh and the Book of Durrow – products of the monasteries of Ireland, which because of its isolation, and perhaps its climate, was not then overrun by hordes of barbarians as was the rest of western Europe.

For the last 25 years, the barbarians have been among us – and worn many guises. We have lived at the edge of civilisation. But the arts and culture – diverse, perceptive and contemporary European – have survived here and prospered. They have done so for a variety of reasons; because they have not been a threat; because with the support of government we have been able to rebuild what was destroyed. But most importantly, they are seen as having an enduring value, dimly seen but nevertheless real, which the diverse elements in our society could all respect.

NOTE
1. John Myerscough, *The Arts and the Northern Ireland Economy* (Northern Ireland Economic Development Office, 1996).

YOUTH AND CULTURAL DIVERSITY IN DRAMA

Michael McGowan

I suppose I should fill you in on some of my personal background which I think is important in a place like Northern Ireland. I originally come from the city of Derry and I use that name purposely. The city is called Londonderry by people who come from another part of it, so you can see already that in my hinterland we suffer from split personalities.

At the moment I live in Belfast, in a district called Ballynafeigh which is just south of the Ormeau Bridge in the city. Some people on one side of this bridge do not want people from the other side to march across it into what they see as their territory. Over the past year I have witnessed the conflict in that part of Belfast. Over the past 25 years I have witnessed the conflict in Derry and Londonderry. I have watched it on the streets and I have watched people constantly shift and redefine themselves

Over the past 25 years, people in Northern Ireland have constantly defined themselves, invented themselves and reinvented themselves both within their own communities and with regard to the other community, be that Catholic, be it Protestant, be it British, be it Irish, be it Northern Irish, be it a redefining the sense of what it is to be Northern Irish. We have seen these processes in poetry, in prose, and in the performing arts.

One of my problems in all of this, working as I do in the Education Unit in the BBC, is that one of my responsibilities is to disseminate these growing and developmental redefinitions. I will tell you one story which is pertinent to what I am saying. I worked with an editor on a series called 'A State Apart' which looked at the history of Northern Ireland from the 1920s until the IRA and loyalist ceasefires in 1994. The editor was 40 years old. As we were working through a lot of material which he had cut as news editor (and working through it with what I consider to be an historian's editorial eye) I noticed that he had not seen the processes which had been in operation here from my perspective. When we came to the programme on the Anglo-Irish Agreement of 1985, I said to him that it could be argued that the politicians are now starting to dictate shifts in people's lives not just politically, but also and ultimately culturally; and that people will start attempting to reappropriate and reinvent their history, so that we were about to go through a very dangerous time, culturally, historically and politically. He said asked me what I meant and I said: 'Let's look at the Anglo-Irish Agreement – did the people accept that or did a section of the people accept that or did the politicians define the agenda on this place?'. What has happened since then is that this society has started to redefine itself again, it has shifted politics onto the streets so that if art and culture are about anything they start from, their first reflection is on the street. When people like Heaney, and our great dramatic writers start analysing, they start analysing from the street. And what we have now in Northern Ireland, 25 years on, is a redefinition of both cultures or traditions which I think is a much more dangerous view of this place than has hitherto been the case. One of the added poignancies about the problems of this place is that we do become obsessive about it. Now that sounds totally obsessive on my part and I do not think like that all of the time which brings me to youth drama.

One of the reasons for this conference is our obsession here with diversity and difference. Donnell Deeny talked earlier about the Arts Council in Northern Ireland and the types of cultures it attempts to reflect. He and his officers in their wisdom gave me £1,000 last year to seed a project which is quite unique. It allowed BBC Northern Ireland to come up with a series called 'Study Irish, English and Drama'. What it allowed us to do, was to send three writers into three different parts of Northern Ireland to encourage kids to tell their own stories. I give them the baggage which I have just declared about myself and what I consider has happened here over the past 25 years. I then chose three writers whom I thought would reflect some of those considerations in their work with the kids. The three writers were Damian Gorman, Gary Mitchell and Rebecca Bartlett, all of whom have a vested interest in the history of this place. Gary Mitchell comes from Rathcoole, had been a member of the UVF and described himself as a community politician in Rathcoole. He became a writer at the age of 27. Damian Gorman has just recently founded an organisation called An Crann which is an attempt to collect the grief of this place through individual experience and stories and put it on record. Rebecca Bartlett is, like the others, totally committed to, interested in and obsessed by the history of this place. So they went to Armagh, Derry and Belfast. I assumed that the kids they were going to work with, who are aged between 15 and 17, were totally obsessed by the Troubles, and this society, which has been redefining itself and reinventing itself over the course of the Troubles. However, what interested those kids were their own life stories, their own sense of themselves. They were not interested one iota in the Troubles, the cultural diversities which I mentioned earlier as being the basis of this experiment. It was a unique experiment in that these writers were not sent to reflect their own agendas but to reflect the stories and the concerns and the issues which engaged those young people.

I would like to show you a clip and I think its important not to forget in all of this that there is a universality of experience which is experienced by children here, by children in France, by children in Spain, Germany, and wherever. All children's experiences are bound to be different but there are, I think, more similarities than differences. I would like to show you just one clip from one of the dramas. It is a script written by Damian Gorman and is essentially a summary of a series of workshops with kids from Orangefield School in East Belfast, from St Louise's in West Belfast and from Victoria College, South Belfast. I chose specifically (because I was producing all three dramas) to be sexist, and asked Damian to work only with girls because my fear was, based on previous experiences, that guys tend to dominate conversations. All of the girls ended up acting in the finished dramas as well. Two of the girls from this group had lost their fathers, killed as a result of the troubles, which did come out in the course of the workshops, and they did work through it. It was a personal issue for them, but, as it was not a group issue, the group decided to reject it as a theme which they would like to investigate through youth drama. What they did come up with was what I considered to be a much more sophisticated drama, and a much more sophisticated theme, to do with a sense of insecurity at a time of their lives when they are about to split from each other. They have to make decisions about careers, about where they're going to next. Also the cafe they gathered in (which gave them a sense of security that they didn't feel at home) was also about to change: it was about to become part of the marketplace philosophy that inhabits the world in which we live in at the moment. You will find none of that language in this drama. The following text is drawn from the first five minutes of the 'Study Ireland' drama.

Mrs McCafferty: So I brought a little bit of Paris to Belfast – everything's French, the ambience, the detail, the music, as you can hear.
Girl: Shit!
Mrs McCafferty: Ooh girl.
Hugo McCafferty: Sorry love.
Mrs McCafferty: Now I knew you were training so I'll make this as easy as I can. Who are you with by the way?
Girl: Well this piece is where the catering review – I'm doing a Media Studies course at Coleraine University.
Mrs McCafferty: Ah – university, university, uh – I never had the time myself – I suppose I'll just have to wait for the Honorary Degree (followed by a chuckle).
Girl: Maybe you could start by telling me how you began all this Mrs McCafferty.
Mrs McCafferty: Café Grande you mean – uh – now there's a story . . .
Girl: I know this woman and I know the story. She doesn't seem to recognise me or maybe she does. Well I've certainly changed and so has this place!
Girl: Hugo McCafferty's café – 'McCafferty's caf' – here was our harbour – here we were safe and sound – a home from home for the fifth year walking wounded – Mo and Diane, Barbara, Louise and me. And who was like us? I'm sure there were plenty like us – nervous wrecks about to sail out into jobs or sixth form life. Things were beginning to get serious in every direction. We all wanted to do well without being too sure of what doing well meant, but it seemed to mean passing exams so you could do more exams, as if you hadn't enough on your plate, just growing up. There were times when your whole life seemed like a series of tests (*clock ticking*): – how do you deal with a mum who wants everything for you, how do you deal with a boy who wants all he can get, how do you spell commitment – with two t's or three? I think Mo was the wisest of all of us or the kindest one anyway. Her parents split up when she was seven or eight and they'd split her brothers and sisters too. Maybe that's why she could always see everyone else's point of view. Louise was the one I always felt sorry for though it was probably stupid. She wasn't shy or anything. She seemed to have a lonely streak. I could have imagined it but I didn't dream of Diane or Barbara's problems. They both got it right in the teeth and especially Diane. Her mother took sick the Christmas before our GCSEs. There was only the two of them at home. At least Barbara had her family.
Hugo McCafferty: Your label's sticking up at the back.

Mrs McCafferty: It's supposed to be sticking up at the back – it's French!

Hugo McCafferty: Have a cup of tea anyway.

Mrs McCafferty: You're a mess!

Hugo McCafferty: I haven't even washed meself yet.

Mrs McCafferty: That's not what I mean Hugo McCafferty. Your business is a mess – your bank statement came in this morning.

Hugo McCafferty: Oh!

Mrs McCafferty: Oh! uh! Is right!

Hugo McCafferty: 'I – I have a plan.

Mrs McCafferty: You've a plan?

Hugo McCafferty: I have.

Mrs McCafferty: Like what?

Hugo McCafferty: Like 'im. Right. I was saying to the girls that we should make the dukebox free to attract a lot more people.

This drama could be translated into a language, really! My assumptions were that these children were concerned with growing up, with peer group pressure; they were certainly not interested in my concerns. One of my problems with that is that one of my jobs is to try to disseminate information about Northern Ireland and part of that is to make assumptions and analyses. The cautionary note I want to give to the conference, is that we should not pass our own obsessions onto kids. I think the history of this place, and the pressure which that history brings to bear on all of us, is the kind of pressure which we can only start to analyse post-secondary school. I have difficulties with it even now. Those diverse historical pressures which have come to bear on Northern Ireland do not come to bear on kids, as evidenced by these dramas. The dramas were not the work of the three writers. They were the work of all the children who took part in the workshops. It is their voice, their statement – and it is a universal statement.

LANGUAGE IN EVERYDAY LIFE

Dónall Ó Riagáin

Europe is a linguistic and cultural mosaic. In the European Union alone about 45 autochthonous languages are spoken by its 368 million citizens. These do not include the many Asian and African languages spoken by recent immigrants and guest workers. There is at least one linguistic minority in each and every EU member state. There are eight in France and no fewer than 13 in Italy. In the UK we find Welsh in Wales, Cornish in Cornwall, Gàidhlig and Scots in Scotland, and Irish and Ulster-Scots in Northern Ireland. In a word, linguistic diversity is the norm, not the exception in contemporary Europe.

The European Union has 11 official, working languages in contrast to two each in the Council of Europe and NATO and six in the UN, a world-wide body. In addition, Irish is a 'treaty language' – that is to say there are authoritative versions of the treaties and other major documents in Irish and Irish may be used in the institutions of the EU, subject to certain conditions. Of course, some languages are more widely used than others. A Eurobarometer Survey[1] carried out in April and May 1994, showed German to be the most common mother-tongue in the EU, spoken by 24 per cent. Italian and English tied for second place with 17 per cent each, and French came close behind with 16 per cent. However, when asked what language, other than their mother-tongue, they knew, more people (25 per cent) stated English than any other language. French with 13 per cent came in second place, and German a poor third with 8 per cent.

Another interesting survey was carried out at around the same time. This one sought to ascertain what languages EU officials really used in their everyday work. It was conducted by the Gerhard-Mercator-Universität of Duisburg, Germany. The findings showed that French dominated both oral and written communications, not only internally, but also between EU staff and the European public. English was a respectable second but German, notwithstanding its very strong position as a mother-tongue, was used in only 3 per cent of oral or written communications with the public and 1 per cent of internal communications. All of the other official, working languages combined accounted for only 1 per cent of communications. The conclusions are clear. While people wish to retain their mother-tongue they are quite happy to use a small number of widely used languages to facilitate international communications.[2]

In addition to those who speak these official, working languages – languages which are the main official languages of the member states – it is estimated that up to 50 million EU citizens speak as mother-tongue, a European language other than the main, official language of the sovereign state in which they live. These people can be listed in five categories:

1. Those who speak Irish and Luxembourgish, the national languages of two countries, which are not among the 11 official, working languages of the EU and which are lesser-used by any standard;

2. Those who speak a language which is in a minority position in the sovereign state in which they live and which is not spoken in any other country. Welsh in the UK, Breton in France, Friulan in Italy and West Frisian in the Netherlands are obvious examples;

3. Those who speak a language which is in a minority position in the sovereign state in which they live and which is in a similar position in another country. For instance, Catalan and Occitan are spoken in France, Spain and Italy;

4. Those who speak a language which is in a minority position in the sovereign state in which they live but which is a majority language in another country. Examples of such communities are the German-speaking minority in the east of Belgium, the Greek speakers of Puglia and Calabria, in the south of Italy, and the Swedish speaking community in Finland; and

5. Those who speak non-territorial European languages, ie the Gypsy and Jewish languages. While these languages have been spoken in Europe for centuries, they cannot normally be said to belong to any particular territory.

While the so called lesser-used/minority/regional languages are not mentioned in any of the EU treaties there has been a growing awareness that the new Europe must be able to accommodate its linguistic and cultural diversity. Europe's history has many examples of strong nations trying, not only to conquer the lands of weaker peoples, but to impose their linguistic cultural and religious values on the conquered peoples. This inevitably led to alienation, resentment and conflict. Happily, diversity is now seen more and more, not as a cause of division, but rather as a source of enrichment.

Language is not just a tool of communication, but much more than that. It is also a vehicle for cultural expression, an instrument developed and honed by a people to give voice to their finest and most intimate thoughts, a custom-built receptacle in which the collective wisdom of a people can be recorded, stored and passed from one generation to another. Just like a species of flower each language is unique and irreplaceable. In this era of urbanisation and depersonalisation is it any wonder that people thirst for a sense of belonging – of identity? It is hard to know where we are going if we do not know from where we came. Knowing and using the language of our ancestors can be the key element in this quest for identity. By the beginning of the 1980s the 'roots phenomenon' was influencing thinking in many international fora. The European Parliament has now adopted four important Resolutions on Europe's lesser-used languages – the Arfé Resolutions 1981[3] and 1983[4], the Kuijpers' Resolution of 1987[5] and the Killilea Resolution of 1994[6]. The Killilea Resolution was adopted by 321 votes in favour, one against and six abstentions – a clear indication of a new climate of tolerance and respect for diversity. The Parliament established an Intergroup Committee for Minority Languages in 1983. This committee is functioning well and meets every month during the plenary session of Parliament in Strasbourg. In 1982 a line was opened in the EU budget for lesser-used languages. There were only 100,000 ecu in it, the first year: it now stands at 3,675,000 ecu.

The 40-member Council of Europe, not to be confused with the EU, adopted the European Charter for Regional or Minority languages in 1992 and accorded it the legal form of an international convention. The Charter has been signed by 16 states and ratified by four – Norway, Finland, Hungary and the Netherlands. When the fifth instrument of ratification is lodged with the Secretary General of the Council of Europe the Charter will come into effect as a convention. I am sorry to say that neither the UK nor Ireland have yet signed the Charter. Other international organisations, notably the OSCE[7] and the UN[8] also have made positive declarations.

The organisation of which I am Secretary-General, the European Bureau for Lesser-Used Languages, was established at a colloquy organised in Brussels in May 1982. It has its general aim to conserve and promote the lesser-used autochthonous languages of the European Union, together with their associated cultures. The Bureau remains independent in matters of party politics, religion, class, race and ideology. It has committees in 13 countries and these are broadly representative of the linguistic minorities living in those states. The Bureau's UK Committee has sub-committees in Scotland, Wales, Cornwall and Northern Ireland. The organisation's head office is based in Dublin and it also has an information centre in Brussels.

The Bureau receives by far the greater part of its income from the European Commission for specific projects. It also receives grants-in-aid for a number of national, regional and provincial governments and gets indirect support (eg free office accommodation, hosting of meetings) from a number of regional and municipal authorities. The Bureau collaborates with the institutions of the European Union (especially the Parliament, the Commission and the Committee of Regions), with the Council of Europe, UNESCO, the UN, the Assembly of European Regions and the OSCE.

The Bureau follows four main strategies in pursuit of its general aim. First, it seeks legal and political support for lesser-used languages. The Bureau has lobbied effectively in the European Parliament and other fora – in the European Parliament on the resolutions concerning lesser-used languages and on the budget line, as well as in the institutions of the Council of Europe for the European Charter for Regional or Minority Languages. It has made submissions to the Intergovernmental Conference on the revision of the Maastricht Treaty and is assisting the Foundation on Ethnic Relations in preparing a set of guidelines on minority languages for the OSCE High Commissioner on National Minorities.

Second, it facilitates an exchange of information and experiences among those who are working for lesser-used languages. The Bureau publishes a newsletter, *Contact-Bulletin*, three times a year in English, German, French, Italian and Spanish. It also publishes booklets, reports, posters and videos. It organises annually, in co-operation with the European Commission, a programme of study visits which enables language activists to visit a language community in another country and learn what they are doing to conserve and promote their language. This year the Bureau is organising its first-ever European Language Day. This celebration of linguistic diversity is primarily intended to raise awareness of Europe's linguistic richness and to promote positive attitudes. A special poster/brochure has been published and there will be events in almost every EU member state.

The third strategy is to provide advice and assistance for those working to promote minority languages. The Bureau's head office alone dealt with 4,000 requests for information and help last year. It promotes networking among language activists and endeavours to assist organisations find funding for projects.

Finally, the Bureau has been involved in establishing and continues to support structures and projects aimed at promoting lesser-used languages. The Mercator Networks, a series of information/documentation centres, are obvious examples. Mercator-Media is based in the University of Wales, Aberystwyth, Mercator-Law and Legislation in Barcelona and Mercator-Education in the Fryske Akademy in Friesland.

Every second year a festival for children, who are receiving their education through the medium of lesser-used languages, is organised in a different region. Even as I speak, the fifth Euroschool – or *Euroschule*, as this one is being called – is being held in North Schleswig in the south of Denmark, and is being hosted by their German speaking minority there. I am happy to report that children from *Gaelscoileanna* are among those who are participating in the games, concerts, visits and other activities.

In short, while the Bureau has an enormous task, it has undertaken it with gusto. But let us turn our attention to Northern Ireland.

Despite what we euphemistically call the Troubles of the past 28 years, I believe that there are clear indications of a desire on the part of a growing number of people in Ulster to explore and rediscover the rich linguistic and cultural heritage of the province. I am happy to see that more and more people are anxious to do this in an open and inclusive manner without any unnecessary political or ideological baggage. May I salute, in particular, the work being done by the Cultural Diversity Group and by the Ultach Trust. When people have been living together for almost four centuries it is inevitable that there be a linguistic and cultural cross-fertilisation. Thus we find a slogan such as *Erin go Bragh* in use by sections of the Orange Order or *Ceol agus Craic* used *ad nauseam* by publicans throughout the south of Ireland, without their having any idea that the word *craic* is not Gaelic but Ulster-Scots. My only point is that neither the publicans, advertising music sessions, nor the Orange Order should have any hang-ups about their linguistic borrowings. What they are doing is perfectly natural in a linguistically and culturally diverse society.

Drawing on what I learned from my contacts with other linguistic communities may I offer a couple of policy pointers which I hope are constructive. First, I believe that both the British and Irish governments should be pressed to immediately sign the European Charter for Regional or Minority Languages, and their parliaments to ratify it soon afterwards. In the case of Northern Ireland, appropriate provisions from Part III of the Charter, should be applied to both Irish and Ulster-Scots. If this could be achieved it would mean that language policy in Northern Ireland could be lifted clear of domestic controversy and placed firmly within the reference frame of widely-accepted European standards.

I also believe that there is a very real need for a major sociolinguistic study to be carried out in Northern Ireland. The 1991 Census contained questions on the Irish language for the first time since 1911. (May I say in passing that the Northern Ireland sub-committee of the Bureau had made a strong case for the inclusion of such questions and seemingly their arguments were heeded.) The returns show some 131,974 persons being able to speak Irish and further 10,029 being able to read and/or write it, while lacking speaking ability. These statistics are remarkably close to information gleaned in a Continuous Household Survey in 1987. While census questions have the advantage of applying to everyone and not just a sample group, they are of necessity sparse. The census language questions do not tell us anything of the attitudes towards language or those questioned, of their degree of active ability nor of the frequency or circumstances of actual usage. This type of information is vital for anyone engaged in language planning. Without proper planning there will never be the required level of political and financial support to implement any worthwhile language policy.

The UK government has made reasonably generous provision for television in Welsh and Scottish Gaelic. Unfortunately, no such provision has been made for Irish in Northern Ireland. I am convinced that this situation could be reactivated at very modest cost by means of collaboration with Teilifís na Gaeilge in the Republic. If Teilifís na Gaeilge could be received throughout Northern Ireland and if the Northern Ireland authorities were to provide a certain number of hours of programming an enhanced service could be made available to Irish speakers throughout the island. Furthermore, such transfrontier co-operation could attract EU funding, thus making additional resources available.

In short, with goodwill and a little imagination a lot can be achieved even in the short-term.

Let me finish by quoting part of the message we received from Jacques Santer, the President of the European Commission, for European Language Day. (I remind you in passing that M. Santer is a Luxembourger and that Luxembourgish is his native language.)

> Raising awareness of this linguistic and cultural diversity is very important and, as president of the European Commission and as a speaker of a lesser used language, I fully support the European Bureau for Lesser Used Languages in organising a European Language Day.

If we allow the number of people who speak minority languages to diminish further an important part of European cultural heritage will disappear forever.

European citizens are privileged to live in a multilingual Union and we must recognise this in order to maintain and respect the Union's cultural diversity. Language is the essence of this diversity.

Together let us build a new Europe, including a new Ulster, united in its diversity.

NOTES

1. Eurobarometer, no 41, European Commission, July 1994.
2. See *New Language Planning Newsletter,* vol 9, no 4, June 1995.
3. Resolution on a Community charter of regional languages and cultures and on a charter of rights of ethnic minorities, 16.10.81.
4. Resolution on measures in favour of minority languages and cultures, 11.02.83.
5. Resolution on the languages and cultures of regional and ethnic minorities in the European Community, 30.10.97
6. Resolution on linguistic and cultural minorities in the European Community, 09.02.94.
7. In particular, Section IV of the Copenhagen Document and the Charter of Paris for a New Europe, (both 1990).
8. Declaration on the rights of persons belonging to national; or ethnic, religious and linguistic minorities, adopted by the General Assembly of the United Nations on 12 December 1992.

THE ROLE OF MUSEUMS IN SUSTAINING CULTURAL DIVERSITY

Tomislav Sola

A curious thing about the museum world, which has been enhanced by the advent of the new information technologies, is that now we can remember not just more and more, but everything which we may ever come to know – perhaps even more than we need to. The last 200 years of rational Cartesian conquest have stumbled into the trap of quantity. It was not the Muses but the nymph Mnemosyne – the goddess of Memory – who gave 'museums' their name. The former name would suggest art and creativity, whereas the latter is more suggestive of a ruthless machine that sees progress as the accumulation of memories. This vision of a society of perfect recall is unfortunately becoming reality in our museums. The only perfectionism museums have been eager to aspire to, besides scholarship (often important for science but irrelevant for everyday life), is an excessive collecting which has virtually become a mania. Thus, while our museums exude quantity, it is nevertheless quality which is important. In other words, how should we select what we put into our museums? This is a process known to museums for ages, but is a question which museum curators for the most part avoid. The questions we should be asking are: what is worth remembering? Which memories will give us some hope? Will any offer us greater freedom and a better future?

I am here for two reasons. First, I represent a large and blossoming profession. After 15 years in museum practice, I am now involved in educating the museum curators of the future. While I do regard theory as extremely important (as it is a concentrated experience of the profession), I still consider myself primarily a practitioner. I say this to avoid giving the impression of proposing grand abstractions. The second reason I am here is that I come from a part of the world very experienced in what you here so nicely term 'the Troubles'. In 'our' war there, we have had a sweeping-away of all diversities in the name of the nation-state ideal. Speaking as a museologist, I am ashamed my profession was not able in that situation to do better than it did. This is why I am fascinated by what you are trying to do here – to keep diversities side by side. This is an enormous and very difficult task but the alternative is tragic beyond imagination. Leaving the domain of politics (if one can ever leave it!) I would like to propose now the thesis that museums will help little in this task – in their present form at least. While they can be relatively good at preserving the identity of a certain community or nation, affirming and defending its uniqueness, they can do little or nothing to deal with the uniqueness of others. This is, of course, a strange way to remember, making a selection in the interest of governing forces, yet lacking an ethical dimension, presenting the museum as a mere tool. But it is the case, almost as a rule, and I am afraid that the institution of the museum as we know it is neither able nor even intended to deal with the problem. I suppose I have now destroyed the need for the rest of my contribution, but since I have the floor, I shall use the chance to dwell upon this impossibility and proffer some possible remedies. How then do we make museums different – open to the problems of the world around them?

Have you ever asked yourself why museums all over the world are almost literally exploding in their development? In Europe a new museum comes into being almost weekly. This is I think because we are all shuttered in whatever we think our identities are. Globalisation and the internationalisation of cultures are epidemic diseases of the human spirit. The post-cultural world will turn cultures into another industry, making us all wandering tourists and visitors in our own cultures. The business that creates politics (as has always been the case) turns all values into the single one of money and power. This in turn creates a global crisis of identity. Museums are, naturally, recognised as a possible remedy as they are, so to speak, our cultural banks, places where identity is stored and from where in crisis we can draw some inspiration. The whole range of museums does this so well that they contribute to this hypertrophied sense of self which leaves no place for any notion of diversity. This is the fatal 'kiss of Mnemosyne', like a curse of obsessive memorising, leaving no space for creative forgetting. On the one hand we have the cry for museums as the mechanisms of protection in a world turning into a supermarket. This makes museums talk of the present day: never have there been more visitors; there is unprecedented media attention; they are prestigious palaces designed by the most fashionable architects. On the other hand we can see that museums care little for

our destiny and for our real-time problems. Faced with the requirement of attracting more visitors, they offer us useless nostalgic stories
which in times of peace and material prosperity provide some kind of
cultural entertainment, but which become tragically useless in times
of crisis, unrest or war. Thus museums have difficulty finding their
proper place in society: it is neither one of scientific aloofness, nor
one of the entertainment business. They should be friendly places of
social living, where, as in the classical world's forum, traditions were
ranged and their qualities praised, where the present was quarrelled
about and where the welfare and well-being of the community were
made matters of public concern. To conclude, we have more and
more museums because, collectively, we know that we have to install
some protective mechanisms necessary for our spiritual and physical
survival. The poor performance of museums merely increases their
quantity, like an illness it is hoped to cure with an increasing quantity
of ineffective pills. Our global informatic mind is paradoxically suffering from a form of hyperamnesia. We can recall the most arcane
trivia about everything, all has been counted and sorted into vast
databanks; but when it comes to ethical questions such as recognising
the right of our neighbour to share the same soil and air, we
shamelessly imitate our uncivilised ancestors and claim it all for
ourselves. Nothing in human nature, some scientists claim, has
changed in the last 150,000 years. Can this really be true? What
about all those great institutions, all those universities, all our science,
and all the polymaths to whom we erect statues in the temples of
Reason!

In any other situation, I would dwell upon this as the source of well-
founded criticism of museum practice and theory. But, being here in
Northern Ireland today, I will not be so irresponsible as to forget what
is happening around us. So let me denounce two social institutions
which have no obvious connection with museums – politics and religion (I say 'obvious' because they are nevertheless powerful enough
to influence decisively the performance of museums and place them
where they think is appropriate – and I shall say nothing about business people, because they are exempt from any moral concerns
although they possess the greatest power and influence of all). I will
not talk about the experience of my part of the world, as it is painful
and the same as everywhere else. As a Christian I find it beyond comprehension that Catholics and Protestants can be divided by the same
religion. No clergy should be partisan, yet some are – not in the way
which could be forgiven as being only human, but clamouring

through the centuries with the same curses and cries for battle as are still to be heard today. This is not the proper rôle of our spiritual fathers. Politics is an old profession. Politicians are self-proclaimed owners of the collective destiny by virtue of the power of their money, their cruelty and their persuasion. They need power and all the emanations of it and will do anything required to obtain it. This, naturally, may mean a war here and there, as their appetites may be confronted by others having similar but conflicting ones. To do this, they transform a population into a mob and manipulate it into a servile giant with enormous power and no sense of judgement of its own. This is best done through the manipulation of history, where they need the help of corrupt scholars and journalists. They provide alibis and legitimacy to the aspirations of the power-holders. Museums are quite a handy tool in which they can present their findings in the form of objective scientific discourse: a popular and yet official seal to the construct. Of course both parties, not to mention the untouchable third of corporate business, need and finance the museums which either support their hatreds and follow their wishes, or tell the unimportant, entertaining histories of times gone by.

Thus, instead of serving the well-being of the population, museums can contribute to the perpetuation of a nationalist delirium. Memorising is conditioned by an endless number of factors and we can never entirely filter out the influence of our own self, our capacities, experiences and interests. Yet, in comparison with history, memory has a basic quality: history is nothing but a changing picture of interests, re-coloured and re-designed anew for each generation. As an 'applied' memory, it is part of the basis of any museum discourse, in any kind of museum. There is ample testimony as to how deceptive history can be what Paul Valéry called 'the most dangerous product of the intellectual chemistry'. 'Events in the past may be roughly divided into those which probably never happened and those which do not matter' (WR Inge). Aldous Huxley called history 'a branch of speculation connected, often rather arbitrarily and uneasily, with certain facts about the past'.

In deciding not to deliver an academic lecture, I was guided by that Latin saying *Hic Rhodos, hic saltire* (Rhodos is here, jump here), which referred to an athlete boasting of his achievements in the games on Rhodes. As a museologist, I must not repeat the error of museums which do not respond to the circumstances around them. If museums are usable, even powerful and necessary mechanisms of society it is no use claiming that there would come their Rhodes where they will

show their importance: it is usually claimed that museums merely preserve cultural relics for future generations. Implicitly, they excuse
themselves for not doing anything substantial for those around them,
by whose taxes they are financed. So they should perform what they
can or should perform, here and now. But most museum curators will
perform any scientific 'salto' to explain that this is not their task.
Why? Because they are reluctant to face up to their responsibility and
they are reluctant to admit that they do not know how to do so. They
can easily handle the big traditional knowledge machine, but it
becomes more and more obvious that the whole thing is wrong as any
museum is a feeble competitor in the knowledge industry. Museums
are transformers: they transform knowledge into wisdom.

A final word on the subject of museums and the sustaining of diversity. Of course they can and do help to achieve this, by the very fact
that they are becoming increasingly aware of their own role in
society. But, as humble servants of their paymasters, they cannot but
follow the mega-trends which are contrary to their inherent interests
and to those of the society they are supposed to serve. One mega-
trend is the transformation of the past into a commodity. For
museums, this means transformation into a heritage industry and
farewell to any ambition of having a corrective role in society. In this
view, diversity will be preserved for generations to come by
museums in their antiseptic, climatised glass cases and by what heritage centres offer in their shops and workshops. One could believe,
though, that there would be a corrective move which will force
even museums to take part in the life of their respective communities,
to serve real people in their real time and to solve their real
problems.

What can the past, stored and interpreted in the museums of
Northern Ireland teach us, to help preserve diversity and peaceful
coexistence? I have not visited a sufficient number to be able to claim
for sure that the choice is not as wide as one would wish: their very
existence is a message already. Professionalism comprises ethical
objectiveness by which museums must serve first the human cause
and not the exclusivist interests of their respective community. If left
to their professional consciousness those museums would have to
make the basic choice first: would they serve hatred or support goodwill? I will give one example of the museum destiny: communist
regimes in eastern Europe fell for a variety of reasons. One was that
they had bad museums (which was not so much a reason for the failure of communism as a sign of it). But the huge network of so-called

'museums of the revolution' was to blame. They were so ill-conceived that they produced hatred instead of tolerance and goodwill. They served death not life, Thanatos not Eros. In the former Yugoslavia, in their indoctrinated one-sidedness and the naive claim that we should still hate Germans and each other (as the opposing sides in the civil war), they obscured the message of peace and blurred the horror of warfare. They were simply too political, serving the increasingly odious Party. Like the Party, they produced hatred and inspired it instead of helping people live in harmony.

One should know that intolerance is created even by uncritical interpretation or glorification of one's own identity. If politicians are happy to build their strategy upon 'either us or them', museums must not be, and this should be clearly told to the community over and over again. The mob as formed by politicians, may require differently, but museums, like the church, should have firm ethical standards. After all, unlike politicians and profit-makers, museums and churches are not meant to be temporal, but calibrated for eternity. Think in terms of eternity and act in your particular time slot. Museums are neither disinterested scribes, nor judges, but rather a conciliatory force stemming from the deep and long human experience of suffering. It is true all over the world, and I believe also in Northern Ireland, that museums are happily dealing with specialist knowledge and particularities only. They do so even when it is obvious that problems of their society, to be solved, require the wise generalist more than the knowledgeable specialist. If museums cannot be of enough help individually, there is a museum community that should be united by the same set of ideals. The museum network is the forgotten value, suppressed by the particular interests of institutions and their irresponsibility. The cumulative force of museums is rarely used and presents a deep well of interdisciplinary experience. Hopefully, information technology, which reaches across different disciplines and scientific categories, will influence museums too.

Therefore, we need the brave and wise among museums. The ideal museum should be based upon the cybernetic notion of balance. It should serve the sustainable development of society, and facilitate change by the elaborate action of corrective impulses. After all, whatever we do, from individuals to nations, we do to survive. To survive means to continue and continuing involves being able to sustain change. Taking part in these processes implies quality which can only be explained in terms of professional knowledge, integrity, responsibility and wide ethical commitment. In short, there is a chance that museums could contribute considerably to preserving diversity, be it Northern Ireland or anywhere else, but they are still extremely weak and vulnerable opponents to all the forces of uniformity and decadence.

MUSEUMS AND CULTURAL DIVERSITY:
A BRITISH PERSPECTIVE

Eilean Hooper-Greenhill

What is cultural diversity in Britain?

The range of cultures, religions, and ethnicities in a society is specific
to that society's history. The present-day diversity of culture in Britain
has a broad spectrum that includes but is not limited to Europe. In
common with many other European countries, Britain has been a site
of transition over many centuries: people coming to Britain have
included Celts, Romans, Anglo-Saxons, Vikings, Normans, Jews,
Huguenots, Poles, Ukrainians, people from Africa, from Asia, and
from the Caribbean. An even greater number has migrated from
Britain, for example to the USA, Canada, New Zealand and Australia.
Much of the mix of people in Britain relates to Britain's history of
empire and colonialism.

At the present time, those living in Britain who have been born outside Britain make up 7.3 per cent of the population: of these the
largest group is of Irish people, who make up 1.5 per cent of the total
population. Other European groups make up 0.9 per cent of the
total. 3.1 per cent of the total population of Britain were born in New
Commonwealth countries (which includes the Caribbean, South
Asia, South-East Asia, and Africa).[1]

On the whole, when the expression 'cultural diversity' is used in
Britain, it refers to those who bear visible marks of difference, in other
words, people from the Indian sub-continent, Africa and the
Caribbean. Sometimes Chinese people are also included. Many of these
groups have come to Britain relatively recently, but many cities, such as
Liverpool and London, have their own long-established black communities that are (generally) living alongside of, but not always part of, the
local working class. 'Ethnic diversity' might be a more accurate expression, and in many ways, the term 'cultural diversity' succeeds the term
'ethnic minority', which is seen as tending towards the pejorative.

At the time of the 1991 census, 5.5 per cent of the population of Britain was described as not white. 1.6 per cent belonged to an ethnic group described as black, 2.7 per cent were from South Asian groups, and 1.2 per cent Chinese and others. Nearly half of these black and Chinese people live in Greater London, where the proportion that identify themselves as belonging to a major ethnic group of non-European origin is approximately 20 per cent.

It is difficult to talk about 'cultural diversity' without very quickly acknowledging issues to do with perceptions of 'race', class and gender. British society is deeply divided along these lines, and over the last 15 years, if a limited number of gender barriers have been broken, many of those to do with race and class have become more strongly established. For many black communities, both those born in Britain and those who have arrived since the Second World War, life is not easy. Stephen Small points out that, measured by just about every major economic and social indicator, black people are at a disadvantage: they are more likely to be unemployed or to be lowly paid, to be living in rented accommodation, and to be less well educated than their white counterparts.[2]

Small uses the expression 'racialised' inequality, to indicate that 'race' is not a biological given, but is a socially constructed set of beliefs and ideas created historically during the colonisation of the Americas. That 'racialised barriers' exist for black people in Britain is documented in statistics and reports such as the recent government (OFSTED) report which shows how, in Birmingham in 1994, 4.6 per cent of black five-year-olds were performing at levels expected of six- or seven-year-olds, 4.6 per cent of black five-year-olds, compared with 3.6 per cent of white children. African-Caribbean five-year-olds outperformed their white peers in both 1992 and 1994 (the only years that figures are available for), and yet, by the age of 16, children are six times more likely than other African-Caribbean children to be excluded from school and in their GCSE exams are on average about five points lower than white pupils.[3] This grim picture of disadvantage is confirmed by research by the Scarman Centre, University of Leicester, that confirms trends at a local level. It further states that a high proportion of black children do not enjoy or like school, and one of the reasons is that there is little material about black history or culture. As one child said when interviewed: 'There's nothing about black people in any of the lessons. I think that is wrong especially as we have to learn things about everyone else.'[4]

Very many African-Caribbean and Asian youngsters face a future of unemployment, especially in some of the inner cities. Many of the older generation are angry and disillusioned. Although the picture is not entirely bleak, many people, both black and white, have been distressed during the last 15 years to see the implementation of social policies in education (reduction of section 11 funding), law and order (introduction of the 'sus' stop and search laws) and the police that have led to a deterioration of race relations. The government's involvement in the 1997 European Year against Racism is viewed with suspicion by both anti-racist organisations and by individuals.

Largely as a result of the social and political situation described above, 'cultural diversity' in British museums is perceived as an issue that focuses almost exclusively on black communities and which is a response to concerns over their position within British society. At the same time, to talk about 'cultural diversity' is to use a language which glosses over the realities of unequal social relations and life opportunities through focusing on culture rather than economics, and diversity rather than disadvantage. There is a further problem with the expression: to refer to something or someone as 'diverse' suggests that there is a 'norm' which is being diverged from. Although I have used the expression in print myself, I am not happy about this aspect of it, although one alternative, 'cultural difference' is also problematic. Perhaps 'cultural pluralism' is an alternative – but language is a problem.

British history and culture

When nearly a century and a half ago, in 1856, the National Portrait Gallery was founded, the stated intention was to draw together a collection of 'likenesses of celebrated individuals . . . whose names stood for the maintenance and development of the whole national tradition'. The first portrait to be collected was of William Shakespeare. The 'whole national tradition' was, as you might perhaps expect, limited to royalty and upper-class and aristocratic men, those who either ruled the country through political involvement, or who were prominent in the arts. This attempt to construct a monolithic and singular view of the world can now be seen as one facet of the modernist project, one of the meta-narratives that were called upon to underpin and validate positions of dominance.

This modernist world-view is still very much in evidence, although on all fronts it is under attack. It permeates British culture, and is still in many ways invisible, even though it is written into the buildings and environments that form our cultural monuments. Clandon Park in southern England is an archetypical British country house, standing as an example of a cultural tradition which is venerated for its elevated taste, sophisticated architecture, and erudite classical references. It belongs to the National Trust. One of its most celebrated features is the ceiling of the Great Hall, described in glowing art historical terms in the National Trust guidebook. One of the hall's main features is the ceiling, where 'extraordinary feats of foreshortening' give us relief sculptures of slaves that are contrived to fall from the ceiling, making a reference for those who can read it to Michelangelo's work in the Sistine chapel. Over the east and west doors are what the guidebook calls 'busts of negroes' that are thought to refer to the Jamaican origins of the Onslow family fortune. The guidebook is not specific as to precisely what activities in Jamaica the family was engaged in, and further research would be needed to find out, but it is well-known that many English fortunes were made in the 18th century from the profits of slavery. The main point to make here is that this casual architectural comment on the processes of colonialism goes largely unremarked today but is mute testament to the deep-seated relations of advantage and disadvantage on which present-day British society has been built. It is precisely these relationships that begin to explain the figures of black school failures quoted above, and it is partly through culture that these relationships are forgotten.

Traditional museum techniques of display tend to decontextualise, drawing objects out of their untidy and confused contexts in the real world into new purer relationships in the museum that tell large-scale stories, stories of imagined communities and of invented pasts, stories, which like Walter Benjamin's angel of history,[5] stand over the wreckage of history, looking into the past but which are hurled into the future, drawing the past and the future together into a compelling narrative of progress that writes out those who because of the depth of their pockets, their gender, or the colour of their skin, cannot take part. Authoritative, large-scale, frequently celebratory, these museum narratives are difficult to contradict; there is no named author, they are legitimised by the power of the institution, their labels and texts state facts rather than suggest interpretations.

Museum display techniques seem designed to isolate the past, to sever the connections to the present and to efface the symbolic references of things. Placing objects in glass cases cuts them off physically from the observer, sets them apart as things to be seen but not understood, and in the minimal labels that name and date the object, its stories are lost. In the absence of the object's own narrative, it is susceptible to incorporation into the fiction of the observer.

There is in Glasgow Museum an American Indian shirt belonging to the days of cowboys and Indians and the Wild West. The film genre of the 'Western', and children's stories and games, perpetuate a romantic myth that conceals the unsavoury processes behind the construction of American democracy. The object's own story, however, once brought to light, reveals a more poignant and brutal set of events, that while appearing to be lost in the past, in fact affect us globally today. It is a particular kind of shirt – a Ghost Dance shirt, thought to protect its wearer from death, but looted from a body at the Battle of Wounded Knee in South Dakota on 29 December, 1890; it was used as part of late nineteenth century 'Wild West' exhibitions and performances, and was given to the museum following Buffalo Bill Cody's Wild West European tour of 1891. It was displayed at Kelvingrove Museum in the ethnography gallery alongside other artefacts from Wounded Knee (a necklace of hide, a pair of buckskin moccasins embroidered with beadwork, and a Sioux cradle). In 1992 the Ghost Shirt was lent to the exhibition Home of the Brave, in Glasgow, where an America lawyer, John Earl, a Cherokee descendent, recognised the shirt. On returning home, he contacted the Wounded Knee Survivors Association, and currently, the museum is engaged in a prolonged discussion over the restitution of this artefact, with many Scottish people feeling that it should indeed go home along with the necklace and other items.[6]

This small case-study serves as a good example of processes that museums are engaged in across the world, and curators in Britain are well aware of events in Canada, Australia, New Zealand and elsewhere. Artefacts that have previously been silent or silenced are being made to speak again, but to tell stories from new perspectives, to make the connections between the past and the present explicit and to expose the contradictory elements that the pure universalist modernist discourse concealed. The deep-seated cultural diversity of British history and society is coming into view as a result. And museums are beginning to be one of the institutions which enable that.

How have museums engaged with 'cultural diversity'?

There is a range of issues which emerge when we consider how museums have responded to the challenge of cultural diversity. One of the most crucial is staffing. Some museums over the last few years have employed staff from specific local communities, and where this has happened excellent and long-lasting links have been built. Cartwright Hall in Bradford is a particular example, where, with an Asian curator of art, relationships with a range of Asian communities are of long establishment. In Liverpool, an outreach officer from the African Caribbean community has been appointed to work with a new permanent display on Transatlantic Slavery. A second issue is the membership of the Board or Committee, where much museum policy is decided. Few have members of different ethnic groups on their strength.[7]

A third issue is how objects are displayed. Some curators are exploring new approaches to displaying objects. At the National Portrait Gallery in London, a small temporary exhibition uses the familiar celebratory approach to celebrate the life of Ignatius Sancho. Very traditional display techniques are used – objects are placed in cases, with small amounts of information given for each of them. However, the choice and juxtaposition of objects is used to make unusual points, as is the choice of words to contextualise the objects.

The contrast between Sancho's birth on board a slave ship and his later acceptance as a writer and composer in British 18th-century society is made evident by the conjunction of slave shackles placed next to a harpsichord. As the visitor contemplates this real but surreal relationship, she hears Sancho's harpsichord music being played. The information given with a portrait of the Duchess of Portsmouth, used in the temporary exhibition on Sancho, highlights the 18th-century custom of having black pages and servants. In the permanent National Portrait Gallery display the label names the sitter and the artist, but ignores the child in the painting: it effectively de-visualises her. A coffee cup is displayed, with comments made on the transfer print, which shows a couple being served by a black servant. Further label text refers to the importance of sugar in British (and European) social life, and the origins of this in the slave plantations in the Caribbean. This places the cup in a social and political context: the frequently-found references to 'creamware' place the cup in a context within the history of design, effectively ignoring other histories.

The exhibition is being used by schools, and is linked to the BBC Black History project through the internet. The *Times Educational Supplement* has been used to alert teachers to the potential of the exhibition. In this exhibition familiar display techniques have been used to reveal previously ignored links between the present and the past, to give new information about some episodes of black history; new technologies have been used as a strategy to broaden the audience and to introduce the project to children.

A number of exhibitions in recent years have been based directly on researching and acknowledging the diversity of British culture. Three that are discussed in my recent book *Cultural Diversity*[8] are Transatlantic Slavery: Beyond Human Dignity, in Liverpool; The Peopling of London, at the Museum of London; and Warm and Rich and Fearless, in Bradford. At the same time, many museum education departments have been working for many years with school groups from inner city schools which are nearly always made up of ethnically mixed groups. Much of the work has been planned with an awareness of the needs of children who may not speak English as a first language, who may live in one culture in school and another at home, or who may have come to Britain as refugees from ethnic struggles. Working in south London, the education department of the Horniman Museum, for example, is sensitive to the environments from which many of their smallest customers come.

This sensitivity has led to some innovative methods of using collections. Vivien Golding[9] has used natural history specimens to illustrate a West African dilemma tale, and I would like to conclude with an example of this. The Museum 'lesson' consists of the telling of the story, and the ensuing discussion with the children of the dilemma over differences that the story presents. This is an abbreviated version of the story:

> One day it rained and rained. The water made bigger and bigger puddles, and rose higher and higher. Squirrel was happy that she had made a nest high up in a tree and was safe. Then she saw her friend Hedgehog. He could not swim, and he didn't have a nest, so Squirrel helped him by letting him come into hers.
>
> That night the friends were very tired and went to sleep exhausted. Hedgehog rolled into a ball, because hedgehogs like to sleep like that, but he took up all the nest, so that Squirrel could not get to sleep. Next morning she told him she didn't like this, and he promised to try to be more careful. The second night Hedgehog tried to sleep on the other side of the nest, but he rolled over and pricked Squirrel so she couldn't sleep again. This went on for some time until finally Squirrel said to Hedgehog that he would have to leave, but Hedgehog said if he did he would

die because he couldn't swim. They decided to build a bigger nest together.

What would you have done?

NOTES

1. M. Brown and J. Hanna, *Roots of the Future: ethnic diversity in the making of Britain* (Commission for Racial Equality, 1996).
2. S. Small, *Racialised Barriers: the Black experience in the United States and England in the 1980s* (London, Routledge, 1994).
3. D. Gillborn and C. Gipps, *Recent Research in the achievement of ethnic minority pupils* (Her Majesty's Stationery Office, 1996).
4. S. Lyle *et al., Education Matters: African-Caribbean people and schools in Leicestershire* (Scarman Centre for the Study of Public Order, University of Leicester, 1996).
5. W. Benjamin, 'Theses on the philosophy of history', *Illuminations*, Fontana Collins, 1970
6. D. Brown, *Bury my heart at Wounded Knee: an Indian history of the American west* (Vintage, 1991).
7. S. Small, 'Contextualising black presence in British museums', in E Hooper-Greenhill (ed), *Cultural Diversity: developing museum audiences in Britain* (Leicester University Press, 1997).
8. See above, note 7.
9. V. Golding, 'Meaning and truth in multicultural museum education', in Hooper-Greenhill (above, note 7).

DIVERSITY: AN ADVANTAGE OR DISADVANTAGE?

Will Glendinning

This morning I really want to consider the question: what effect do the various divisions in society have on the understanding of the cultural diversity which exists in Northern Ireland? The contention I shall put forward is that our understanding of cultural diversity can exist in one of three ways. First, it can exist where culture itself is the root of the conflict. Second, it can exist in a situation of cultural apartheid. Third, it can exist where there is a recognition of plurality, and diversity of cultures as, for example, in Northern Ireland.

In the first of these ways, cultural identity is seen as part of the conflict, used as a political or even an intimidatory weapon, which relates to a whole series of activities. For example, there is the continuing problem of contested marches in Northern Ireland. You will be aware that there have been arson attacks on churches and on halls (Orange halls for example) which would be seen as part of the religious or political identity of one community or the other. The ownership of a particular structure which is a part of someone's territory or culture makes it an object of attack. And the explicit awareness and description of culture can in fact be a means of perpetuating the conflict. This became more prevalent when the IRA ceasefire occurred, as if the absence of IRA violence during that period meant that the conflict which still existed would merely appear somewhere else, and appear more openly in forms of the aggressiveness of cultural identity and the use of it as a way of moving forward a political message. This has resulted in the situation where people wishing to promote a particular cultural identity have to be careful as to how it is used, or may be used, as a political weapon. This is not exclusive to Northern Ireland: the state authorities in Québec have powers to ensure that French is predominantly the language used in the business community there.

The second way in which we can understand cultural diversity, which may be more common than the first, is in a situation of cultural

122

apartheid: that is, where the existence of the differing cultures is accepted but they are seen as being totally separate. Each group wants to describe culture as part of its identity, but exclusively so. And there is almost a vying between people from different backgrounds and traditions to say, if they have that, we must have something similar. This argument comes down to a position of dual provision – if *they* have support for the development of the language, so must *we*. That may be an oversimplification but is nevertheless often the way these things are dealt with, when culture is part of an exclusive identity. The other culture or cultures are seen as alien or carrying a political agenda while one's own culture is not seen as threatening or exclusive. This is a dangerous position as it can easily be a precursor to the use of culture as a weapon in conflict, and indeed, one can set up culture as a target. If there is not room for learning about the complexity of identity, then this type of apartheid can come about. If there is support but no challenge then the increase in knowledge of one culture can be at the exclusion of the other. While a learning process about one's 'own' cultural identity raises questions inside that culture, about what was thought an alien or 'other' culture, the difficulty of where one goes to find out about those issues arises.

I shall cite as an example of this an experience of my brother, who like me comes from a Protestant, middle-class background, and who had an interest in learning the Irish language. One of the things which kept him back was the thought of where he would have to go to do so: he would have to go into Catholic West Belfast, where he might be taught by someone with a republican background who perhaps carried that political baggage into the teaching of the language. His was not the view of someone to whom West Belfast was alien, since he had run my election campaign there and knew the area well, but from someone who wanted to reach out – but who still had that fear. How much more difficult it must be for someone coming from a totally alien position. As it turned out, he started learning Irish in Newtownards, which as many people will know is scarcely a heartbed of the Irish language. However, my brother also told a story of waiting in the queue and being approached by a man who asked if it was the queue for the Irish language class. When told that it was, he ventured that he was a Protestant – and everyone in the queue replied that they were as well. It is that hesitancy to step across into what is seen as the other side's territory which can make it very difficult for people actually to learn about the cultural diversity which exists in Northern

Ireland. This is something of which those involved in promoting the idea of this diversity are well aware.

I would like to mention at this point a piece of research which the Community Relations Council carried out, with the Central Community Relations Unit and the University of Ulster.[1] This research looked at segregation and division in a rural area. (The villages named, by the way, are different from the actual villages.) It looked at two villages and examined where people go to carry on various forms of activity. The villages are only a mile and a half apart, one is predominantly Protestant and the other predominantly Catholic. There is no physical interface between them. But when you look at where people go, you see a mirror image. For example, shopping, entertainment, visiting the doctor and so on, in mainly-Protestant Glendale, people would head northwards to Portadown, Markethill and Banbridge. Markethill is a small local town with one furniture store and one electrical store. Newry, which is a larger district town, would have a much larger number of alternatives for the shopper, yet one finds a higher proportion of shopping for comparable goods in Markethill – 67 per cent, but hardly any in Newry. The other village, Whiteville, shows the reverse. Everyone there travels southwards. This survey was carried out during the IRA ceasefire and at a time when the country was experiencing more willingness on the part of people to travel into other areas. But this shows that, consciously or unconsciously, part of the process whereby people in Northern Ireland decide to go to obtain something, to shop or for entertainment, relates to the issue of cultural or sectarian identity. So how much more difficult it is for people to go and learn about the other cultural identity.

To give two other small examples: in the area I am talking about in which I also live, a neighbour was discussing cinema-going with another person who was totally unaware that there is a cinema in Armagh since he looked totally towards Newry. Half a mile down the road, you would find the opposite. That shows the position moving from a Protestant area to a Catholic one. Further, it reflects a change which has occurred only in the last 20 or 30 years, in a whole series of patterns. As another example, in the same area in the 1950s and 1960s, a lot of young Protestant people would have gone to school in Newry. From the village of Bessbrook, which is very near Newry, Protestants now go to school in Banbridge or Armagh, much further away. Schoolchildren of 11 years of age are getting buses at 7.30 in the morning to go to school. Similar things happen 'the other way round', with regard to Catholics and Protestant areas. Yet when one looks at policy statements of agencies involved in delivering services inside Northern Ireland, there is no mention of these sectarian divisions and how they affect delivery policies. This again can affect the issues of cultural identity and cultural diversity across the area because the net result of this type of problem is that some communities feel marginalised, that services are being withdrawn from them, that they are being pushed out of certain areas. It adds, for Protestants, to the theory that there is a movement to reduce their involvement and deny their cultural identity, and this is reflected in the divisions in the Orange Order between those prepared to negotiate and those against negotiating because they feel negotiation is bound to result in a diminution of their stand.

Those are, I think, some of the problems which we have got to look at. But the more positive side is that we are not aware of the diversity which exists within our own society. For example, let us look at how across district council areas, we celebrate – or do not celebrate – our patron saint. I was taught as a child, and with all sincerity, that St Patrick was not only a Protestant but also a member of the Church of Ireland. The reasoning was that he had to be a member of the Church of Ireland, because he was our saint. Hence one of the difficulties about celebrating St Patrick is: how can we all celebrate him in this country? If 'they' have him, then 'we' do not, so he cannot be 'ours'. If one side claims something the other will move away from it, so that even where the assumption is that everyone celebrates St Patrick, it can become an almost exclusively Catholic or nationalist activity, as some of the celebrations supported or carried out by district councils are seen to be. There can be an 'open' celebration where cultural diversity is recognised, and while in the planning and setting up of these activities, particular trouble is taken to ensure that people from both unionist and nationalist traditions and all the churches are involved, along with people from different bands, organisations and backgrounds. This engenders a richness, a greater ownership and knowledge of the patron saint, and indeed the creation of relationships across the divide.

In other places there is no celebration of the patron saint. His existence is hardly acknowledged in some district council areas. I would suggest that we are faced with the dilemma that cultures can either clash or enhance. At the moment, our cultures are inclined to clash, and that is a very daunting position. Edna Longley[2] has described Northern Ireland as a 'cultural corridor' in which there is a lot of diversity while at either end of that corridor a group of people who have political agendas and identities are trying to block the doors to ensure that what goes on in it does not seep out into the rest of the community. At one end are nationalist groupings, and at the other, unionist groupings. This is so that the purity of their arguments may be maintained.

I would like to finish by pointing out that there is a recognition that diversity exists, but that it does not necessarily mean a reduction or diminution in cultural identity. At Irish dancing classes in the Tí Chulainn Centre in Mullaghbawn somebody said that he was glad to be there as he would be learning some real, true Irish material. The teacher replied that one of the dances to be taught was called 'The Lancers', which had been imported into Ireland by soldiers of the British Army at the time of the Napoleonic Wars. He then gave a list of activities which the questioner saw as Irish but which had as many British or European connections – and this the questioner found decidedly disturbing, as his purity was being challenged.

Other complexities are revealed when you attend a rural Twelfth of July parade and look at the townland names on the banners of the lodges as they pass. These parades are seen as part of Northern Ireland's Protestant British heritage, yet virtually every banner has on it the anglicisation of a Gaelic townland name. The Orange Order is in fact a decidedly Irish institution, in its activities, its way of functioning, and lots of the material that it uses. Consider also the way English is spoken here, with either Irish or Scots phraseology. I am aware of this through my farming pursuits. On my farm are 'tups', or rams. This word appears in Robbie Burns' Lowland Scotland. I have 'sheuchs' and ditches – these ditches are the heights and not the drains. I have sheep which develop mastitis which is called 'fennel', and the udder of a ewe is called an 'elder'. All these are words used regularly by farmers across all backgrounds and areas. People do use these words regularly, no matter from which tradition they come, unaware that the words show the mixture making up our society.

I will end by quoting my brother again. He described a vision I would like to see us able to work towards:

Ulster is often said to be at a crossroads, as if we were for ever poised in uncertainty beneath finger-posts demanding irrevocable decisions and threatening dire consequences. But crossroads are meeting places as well as points of departure and taken in that sense, my homeland is a crossroads of extraordinary interest and diversity. Here meet the English, Lowland Scots, Gaelic Irish and Gallic Scots, and with them they have brought their languages, music, traditions, religion, customs, industry and politics. What we have inherited is as varied as our skies and the patchwork of our fields. I am greedy; I want the lot. I refuse sole membership of either of the two communities to which political theory assigns me. I am not going down any of the roads indicated in those finger-posts. I am going to sit here and let all their traffic come to me.[3]

NOTES

1. Brendan Murtagh, 'Community and conflict in rural Ulster', research summary, University of Ulster.
2. Edna Longley, 'Opening up: a new pluralism', *Fortnight*, November 1987.
3. Robin Glendinning, 'Cultural crossroads, *CRC News*, no. 17, September 1994.

ART: A MIRROR TO DIVERSITY

Brian Kennedy

This paper is not intended as a reasoned discussion on a particular issue. Instead, it is an airing of certain things in one's mind. Like most museum curators I work both as a professional in my own subject of art history, and as a curator of art. Sometimes as you know such a division of labour can cause conflict, although for a lot of the time the two activities are complementary. At the moment both art history and museological practice are undergoing radical change and reassessment, a form of revisionism, as it were, and changes which are coming about in each subject complement one another. For these reasons in this paper I would like to move to and fro between the two subjects; moreover, as we know, art acts as a sort of mirror to society and as in many respects museums can be seen as the polished surface upon which that reflection takes shape.

Our world is changing. The world of art is changing, museums are changing, diversifying, and we must find ways of coping with and adapting to these changes. To my mind the issue confronting us is not one of either accepting change or resisting it, as I think many people still believe to be the case. It is a fact of life and we must face up to it. Saying this though is the easy bit and I am not suggesting for a moment that we abandon attitudes and ideals, methods and techniques which have stood us in good stead for a long time. But we must face the facts. For example, new technology is available to us, to help us in our daily work, but increasingly it is beginning to dictate to us how we go about that work. If asked to state in a word the simple problem for art history I would say it is to communicate, explain or account for that which artists have done, and I would give the same answer to that question asked about museology, except to say that museums must display material, and in so doing must interpret it. I am not particularly well-informed about the new computing technologies and like many people I was for a time hostile to them. What can a computer do that a good card-index can not? But in the

128

early 1980s I had a sort of Pauline conversion, on seeing what a two-minute phone call from the Belfast Central Library's humanities section to the humanities index in California could turn up. Since then like many of us I have become increasingly computerised and I now could not do my work without the new technology.

That we live in changing times is recognised. Yet the nature of the changes we face is difficult to state and quantify. The reasons for change are difficult to understand. Too often we see that all we can do is react – rarely can we determine events. Change seems to be driven by some sort of force and perpetual motion. In very broad terms, concepts such as enlightenment, romanticism, modernism, post-modernism come to mind. In lesser terms we speak of socioeconomic policies, educational needs, heritage and cultural awareness. And of course of the growing diversity within all of these. It is my belief that the broader terms shape the nature and character of the lesser, which come about as a response to them. Such broad changes affect all aspects of life and seem to be supranational and mutual. Thus for example the Enlightenment led inexorably to such things as liberal democracy, although it also led to totalitarianism in its various forms: participation by the masses in the daily events of society, mass education, the establishment of those institutions including museums and art galleries, the proliferation of universities, all of which society considers necessary for the execution and well-being of its affairs.

This chain of events leads inevitably to the need for a set of values through which things can operate. But values do not exist in a Platonic sense; they do not remain static nor are they everlasting as we often seem to think. Rather, everything operates in a given context. This fact in turn leads to the *Zeitgeist* or spirit of an age, a term which as often rejected by historians but one which refuses to go away. The idea of value is contained within it with the implication of a long line of tradition in evolution, yet many of the values which we cherish are in fact 19th century in origin. The museum and art gallery movement is a good example, art history as a discipline is another, and both are the result of developments in areas such as industrialisation, commerce and empire, mass education, the growth of travel, to name but a few. As sets of values develop in society, a canon also emerges – a literary canon, an artistic canon. The latter usually is taken to refer top the time from the Renaissance to the late 19th century, Giotto to Cézanne. Such canons determine our priorities and policies. Thus we come to speak of 'proper' (whatever that may be) scholarship, museological attitudes, practice. In reality, a strictly limited way of looking at things emerges to form a sort of high art which is usually élitist and self-perpetuating. Upon such canons, policies are constructed which eventually dominate our lives. Thus, when we talk so often of things like 'maintaining standards' and so on, we are doing no more than paying homage to a canon of values which almost certainly is of later provenance that we may recognise. And if we do think about the matter, questioning if there was ever a golden age, a time when the canon was established, which if one presses the matter logically must have been a period of thought unsullied by external considerations, political or otherwise, then the answer must be of course that such a time never existed. In terms of art history, for example, can one even imagine what would constitute such a period? Put thus the idea is clearly nonsense. Yet it is one to which we cling.

It is attitudes such as these that our present age questions and this is no bad thing. In almost every sphere of life the canon appears inadequate and no longer satisfies us. Not that the canon was never an established body of knowledge, but as such a body it was all the time wrong, for it served a purpose. Both society's needs and expectations change, and our activities, canon or no canon must adapt to satisfy new circumstances. Thus, again in museological parlance, we watch at the present time as the high culture of a pure and self-contained art cedes ground to a concern for the object seen in its social context. In fact, the primary issue is no longer the work of art itself, rather it has become society. In many fields there can no longer be to the contemporary eye a consensus of what is significant. For us, truly, a diversity, a multiplicity of views is in currency at the same time. This development can only enrich our understanding of things, familiar or otherwise.

This, rather simplistically explained, is the situation in which we find ourselves and art as a discipline, as well as museums, finds itself caught up in it. Furthermore, as an increasingly leisure-oriented society develops, the arts, and in particular museums and art galleries, find themselves for the first time ever in the forefront of both interest and concern. The frequently-heard accusations of élitism, raised at the expenditure of National Lottery monies on such things as the Tate Gallery's new Museum of Modern Art, the Royal Opera House, and other frequently-called 'palaces of the middle classes' are a case in point. The obverse of the coin bemoans the slow passing of things like the Net Book Agreement, arguing that its demise will lead to an unwanted proliferation of merely popular publications to satisfy the masses. Yet, to take a further example of the market catering for mass appeal, the advent 30 years ago of the package holiday has done more to change attitudes, not to mention eating and drinking habits, that any number of official policy documents. Yet in all this I find much to be optimistic about, for change also brings opportunity, and we have initiative, this we can grasp.

Let me look now at some of the issues presently affecting art as a discipline and museums – the mirror – as they interact one with the other. Perhaps the central issue facing art in all its forms – literary, visual, and so on – today is diversity. The canon, as we have seen, has been challenged, the centre (to use a cliché) has given way to the periphery. In short, a form of democratisation has descended upon the subject as a mass of popular culture has come to embrace us. On reflection, from the mid 19th century, from the time, say, of the French Impressionists, such a democratisation has been visible in the arts as subject matter increasingly reflected the common experience. The development of realism and naturalism in both literature and the visual arts were part of this movement and helped us to see an often mundane world in popular and even nostalgic terms. But the process has accelerated this century and now moves with alarming speed. Indeed we have now reached a stage where we believe, being reasonably assured of the development of a subject over time, that we have adopted a reflective stance, turning our attention on the process of how we comprehend our subject, our culture and what it means to us. It is a growing diversity of perception and expectation which is driving this development and this extends, of course, well beyond the borders merely of the arts.

Let us look in detail at some of the issues facing us. Art and museums often share or mirror a common audience, usually middle-class and overwhelmingly composed of social groups ABC1. But such individuals, when visiting museums or looking at art works do not always see the same things, even when looking at the same objects. Art has an aesthetic aspect just as an audience has a social aspect. Museums necessarily communicate with audiences within a social context. Aesthetic ideas therefore are communicated within a given social context even though they themselves may be the product of a different period or context. All this may seem obvious, yet in it is contained a fundamental problem of understanding and interpretation. This is also a problem the new technologies are addressing, not least in the fields of art history and museum studies. In studying the art of any period, whether in a museum or not, most people would agree that it is important or even vital to understand that art in terms of its immediate context, that is in terms of the times in which it was produced. Of course, other than with one's own contemporaries this is an impossible undertaking, though we must nevertheless seek to try. But how can we ever know the past even if we try to immerse ourselves in it by reading novels, examining newspaper and exhibition reports, all the paraphernalia of things emanating from the time? Even if we exhaust all such information we can only approach it in the present. At best therefore, our views of the past are hypothetical and our understanding of it approximate. Such an approach, that hitherto of the canon, implies that the past is a concrete entity which somehow we can try to re-create. But the past is no such thing. It is merely an amalgam of the experience of the times and of the collective ideas or even nostalgia which we have for it. Moreover, works of art are not hermetically sealed or self-sufficient objects. How can we meaning-fully speak of understanding works of the past? If an artist wishes to paint a landscape which is laden with various historical associations, for example, the problem is compounded. That artist cannot avoid bringing a personal interpretation to bear on that landscape, but we, a generation or two later, when we look at this painting of a landscape will bring our own interpretations to bear on it. It will have a reso-nance for us which it did not have earlier. At each stage therefore the work is riddled with quotations and influences of every kind. Our comprehension of a painting is possible only through our reading of that painting, yet that which results from any reading is the conse-quence of the cross-fertilisation of all the images and texts which we bring to it. Literary critics are familiar with the problem. In the words of Julia Kristeva[1], when we read a text, a structure is generated in relation to another structure – in fact, she argues that an image is a 'structuration', an apparatus which produces and transforms mean-ing. Thus an image is understood in relation to another image. It is what is often referred to in literary terms as an 'intertext'. It can and often does act as a sort of siren to tempt us towards something which has another significance and Irish studies perhaps above all are deeply caught in this web.

But where in all this can the truth, irrespective of interpretation, be found? The answer is that it can never be found. There is no such thing. Instead, we are often confronted with what is called the human condition, as for example the Belgian artist René Magritte pointed out in a witty series of paintings under that title produced in the 1930s. As always, we are prisoners of our own times and experiences. This is one of the verities of life that artists understand well. And it is one of the things about art which gives it a universal relevance. As spectators of art it gives us the chance to see ourselves in a broad sociohistorical context. But, paradoxically, it is not something amenable to precise definition. This is the problem for museologists. Hitherto curators have in the main taken the traditional paths of elucidation and explanation, the canonic view, to lay before the spectator an account of the truth of what artists have done and what art is about. Art history as a discipline has pursued a chronological path of description, analysis and discussion. All of this has been necessary of course, but we have now arrived at a stage in museology and art history where social change and increased expectations force us to begin to analyse our methods and conclusions. In short, revisionism is at work here as well. This is no bad thing as it allows us in the process to cast more penetrating interpretations on well-worn themes. New tools at our disposal include the new technologies, and at least in this country, the growing emphasis on interdisciplinary study. Such an approach has long been the accepted way of doing things in some European countries such as Germany. But here, art studies have for too long been considered in isolation and thus too much emphasis has been placed on narrative at the expense of technique and method. The possibilities of the new technologies are playing their part in this. My own institution, the Ulster Museum, is an interdisciplinary museum, with divisions representing the arts, the sciences, and human history. Its origins extend back to the early 19th century when it was solely concerned with collections from the natural sciences. The 1890s saw the addition of collections of both fine and applied arts. Thus we have always thought of our activities, even within the art division, in interdisciplinary terms. In matters museological this has been a bonus, even if in terms of past history it has at times created conflicts of interest and loyalty. But, importantly, in adopting such an approach, we are able from time to time to examine familiar objects in diverse and unfamiliar settings. Thus the temptation to stereotype is reduced.

A coherent philosophy of display is central to the operations of any museum. Traditionally, exhibitions of art have been structured in schools of painting, for example the 17th-century Dutch, or the Enlightenment in England. Within such displays the spectator has relative freedom of manoeuvre to study the pictures with only a minimum of labelling or other textual material to divert his attention. In such displays the pictures are paramount in importance. The individual, a mere observer, is left to his or her own devices. Museums in many countries, especially Germany, still adhere to such an approach, but in this country and others such displays are increasingly seen as élitist with an implied arrogance on the part of the curator, and therefore in politically correct times undesirable. So in their place we have developed tightly structured and highly didactic displays in which, by means of copious labelling and a multitude of text panels, the spectator is led around the gallery from picture to picture, in an often predetermined manner, which is considered to produce a correct or at least acceptable reading of those pictures. Yet despite the questionability of why the reading may be correct or acceptable, the viewer is presented with a plethora of information which often can come between him and the pictures he has come to study. The logic of the curator's well-intentioned approach is clear, but frequently its implications can be problematic. It is a little like requiring the reader of a novel first to read the critics, then the novel, and finally to make up his mind on the matter. Yet I do not mean to denigrate this practice – I indulge in it myself – but rather to point out that for everything there is a price to pay. All this is coming about at a time when museums in many countries are developing a quasi-business ethos with mission statements, business plans and other paraphernalia of the market-place. Usually, or perhaps always, the intention is to broaden the appeal of the service rendered by the institution, yet paradoxically, instead of giving more freedom to the spectator, if not thought out carefully such displays may in fact limit his or her room for manoeuvre and interpretation.

Practices such as these are often introduced in the name of education although they are in effect little more than narrative displays which purport to explain a single truth. Yet as we have seen we live in a time which no longer believes in the concept of a single truth. So, often such displays provide a simplified viewpoint shorn of the myriad reasons (in the context of this conference, I am tempted to say diverse reasons) why a work of art may have come into being, and steer the individual away from the business of studying for himself or herself the work in question. But museums are also nowadays beset with the problem of having to increase their visitor numbers and this too is often exacerbated by the move towards commercial operations, so that the pressure to adopt a narrative approach to displays is at times irresistible. One of the central problems now facing curators therefore, is how to appeal to a wider audience while leaving the individual free to interpret the displays for himself. In any new development the spectator must be given sufficient opportunity to think for himself. The most recent developments in museums and in contemporary art history and related disciplines such as literary theory have seen a marked shift of attention away from the object and towards the spectator. And without spectators there would be no museums. This is a cause for optimism for the act of looking at a work of art is akin to a journey of self-discovery and in the process we learn much about ourselves. The curator must therefore seek to arrange displays which attempt to identify the original problems addressed by the artist and at the same time to present their relevance to contemporary life. Perhaps emphasising the reflective rather than the narrative nature of the work is the key here and hence to our engagement with it. As spectators, in studying and analysing our conclusions before works of art, and in comparing them with the conclusions of others, and of previous periods, we learn both about ourselves and our predecessors, even though we are caught, as we have seen, in a form of intertext. What we like to call truth, therefore, can be seen as the sum of the multiplicity of and diversity of interpretations which can be derived from, or placed upon, any object. The real problem facing us is not one of eliciting the truth, for the truth does not exist in the singular form, but is rather one of understanding meaningfully, in terms of our own society and times, the contribution made by the work before us, and there is no neutral means of painting, no way of depicting it except in a certain style. The traditional approach to museum displays, and to art history, largely ignores such things in an attempt to confront the spectator with the work in a manner which plays down its own rhetorical role; regardless of how a painting has been produced it will unavoidably contain elements of other paintings, and in viewing it we are influenced by other images. Even creating new ways of depicting, and hence looking at, the world, the artist forces us to view earlier ways in which it has been seen. As the American art historian Diane McCleod[2] has pointed out, the relationship between art and society, and, one might add, museums, is a matter of negotiation between biased viewpoints. In her words:

> Art's internal dialogue with art does not take place on a plateau above these proceedings, but forms a vital part of a more expansive discourse. The interplay between aesthetic and social components demonstrates that while ideology is enshrined in artistic practice, that practice also directed the reach of ideology. In this nexus of meaning, all shades of interpretation are woven together in their mutually dependent explanation.

If this is so, how then can we pretend to understand and display a work of art as previous generations understood it? What is the reality of the piece? Is it meaningful, we must ponder, even to ask such a question?

The argument as outlined is, as I have said, an optimistic viewing of the restraints imposed upon us by the human condition. To many observers these constraints presage pessimism, but this is a luxury we just cannot afford. In any case, art will take its own course, it will not be trapped or strait-jacketed into any single mode of thought. Always, and fortunately, museums must adapt to art and not vice-versa. It is in this area of the subject that the new technologies are coming to our aid. We in the Ulster Museum know this well from experience. And one of the things that computerisation forces on one is the need to create structures, hierarchies of information, a thesaurus of terms and so on, which can be used consistently. To the uninitiated this may seem but a matter of detail, but it is akin, for example, to the standardisation of the spelling of words. We hope to build up a compilation of all our exhibits and perhaps make it available much more widely, perhaps using the new technology of the Internet.

There are currently a number of art history projects in preparation, which when ready, will revolutionise the dissemination of information and our understanding of it. Moreover, a major effect of these programmes even now is to accelerate a breakdown of the accepted canon to which I referred earlier. The Getty Art History Project in Los Angeles and the Scuola Normale Superiore in Pisa are at the heart of many of these developments on a world-wide basis and are helping to co-ordinate all aspects of them including the development of commonly-agreed technology, hierarchies of information, hardware, software and so on. The National Galleries in both London and Dublin have much of their collections on disc and visitors can interrogate them as to schools of painters, individual painters and their works or even details of their works. But in each case everything is confined to the gallery's own collection, although the Van Eyck project, instituted at the Netherlands Institute for Art History at The Hague together with the Courtauld Institute in London and Trinity College, Dublin, is aiming to link a number of separate databases, each held with the sponsoring institution, which contain both textual material and visual images of individual artworks. This project, in which I myself have been involved at the periphery, is about to go on trial in an attempt to catalogue holdings of these institutions so that they can eventually be accessed by outsiders. It is my hope that the holdings in the Ulster Museum will be accessible, perhaps through this project, one of the few such projects to be concerned with Irish art. I could also mention the Alberti project, undertaken by a group of scholars from Italian and English universities. Named after the 15th-century painter and sculptor, Leon Alberti, this project has gone further than any of the others I have mentioned to take three-dimensional computer models of mainly Renaissance buildings and to analyse their structure or even to complete unfinished buildings. These computer models also allow one to walk around the building and to experience a sense of space. The same principles have been applied to selected paintings in order to turn two-dimensional objects into three-dimensional spaces through which one can walk. Thus our understanding of perspective, the play of light, the relationship of space and form, are enhanced beyond anything a physical model could provide. In this context one is tempted to regard the actual painting as merely the virtual painting. At the base of many of these schemes is the idea of direct interaction between the spectator and the artist. This brings me back to the ideas of concept, interpretation and explanation which a museologist must confront when creating displays. All of this activity is moving away from a fixed view of things, literal or metaphorical, and hence the canon is further undermined. The Internet too, will take many of these things in its stride and change utterly our perceptions and expectations. The legal and moral issues, not to mention copyright, and the ability to download and reproduce images hitherto protected are other issues to be resolved.

Finally, as I said at the beginning, I feel optimistic about these developments for they are largely consumer-led, a response to the diverse needs of our own age. The art museum has become part of the process of art, a fact recognised since the opening, in the 1970s, of the Pompidou centre in Paris, which was not only an artistic event but also a political statement. We are in effect witnessing the development of culture on demand, for as Declan McGonagle of the Irish Museum of Modern Art has said, the contemporary museum is not a place, but a function.

NOTES

1. Julia Kristeva, quoted in Michael Worton and Judith Still (eds), *Intertextuality: Themes and Practices* (Manchester, 1990, p. 7).
2. Diane Sachko Macleod, 'The dialectics of Modernism and English art' in *British Journal of Aesthetics*, vol. 35, no. 1, January 1995, p. 13.

RICHNESS IN DIVERSITY

Maurice Hayes

I thought I would begin by reading you a poem of Gerard Manley Hopkins, called *Pied Beauty*:

> Glory be to God for dappled things –
>   For skies of couple-colour as a brinded cow;
>   For rose-moles all in stipple upon trout that swim;
> Fresh-firecoal chestnut-falls; finches wings;
>   Landscape plotted and pieced – fold, fallow and plough;
>   And all trades, their gear and tackle and trim[1]

This poem makes an eloquent plea for difference, diversity, the uniqueness of individual things and their contribution to the whole. Hopkins sees this from a theological point of view, as the face of God in creation, the richness reflective of the infinite variety of the Creator. The case can be argued, if less effectively, in humanistic terms as well. Although Hopkins takes a theological stance, the merits of diversity can be argued in political and social terms as well. Since the essence of the market is choice, modern economic systems would not work without the existence of difference and diversity. Although choice can be trivialising, as you can see from the choices offered by our television stations, nevertheless it is better than the cold hand of cultural conformity, imposed for example in the former eastern European dictatorships and elsewhere. Difference, the right to differ and to stand out from the crowd, to contribute from one's own eccentric and iconoclastic position, is one of the bulwarks of a functioning democracy.

What I would like to explore briefly with you is the triple thesis that man needs the support of his own cultural identity and tradition, that a society benefits from a diversity of inputs and that there needs to be sufficient coherence to keep the whole thing from falling apart. In the sense of shared values – is it to be culture or anarchy? Or can the

138

two co-exist: difference and deference? What sort of political or constitutional envelope is required to contain them? One thing which is almost certain is that it is unlikely to be the nation state. This model traditionally required conformity as a central organising principle, an eliding of difference whether of language or lifestyle, and subscription to an enabling or unifying national myth.

It may be though that the model of the nation state, dominant in Europe for the last four centuries, and which was the cause of much bloody warfare, is coming to an end, although the signals are contradictory. Europe on the one hand is moving towards federalism of a sort, but at the same time, old atavistic nationalisms and fears are being revived. Britain resiles from Europe, Scotland and Wales try to assert their separateness from England. Countries which once were strongly centralising, such as France and Spain, have discovered new force and new power in their regions. The region can in fact be seen as the motor of growth in the new Europe, often more significant than the state – look at Catalonia, Lombardy, Rheinhessen. On the other hand, further East, the former Soviet Republics are re-establishing themselves as independent entities, and the tragedy of what was Yugoslavia is clear to see.

On a world stage, economic units have become larger and larger, transcending and making a nonsense of national boundaries as the world shakes out into three or four large trading blocs. In addition, the resources and activities of the organisational power of many multinationals transcend those of about three-quarters of the member states of the United Nations.

There is also a growing recognition of the importance of what are known as 'third generation' rights, following on from the two basic human rights categories of the United Nations system: civil and political rights, and those known as economic and social rights. Most Third World countries see this latter category as more important. In Africa, for example, people are more concerned to be fed than to be kept out of jail. I was talking recently to a man from Yugoslavia who had been visited in Sarajevo by the ombudsman from Austria, who suggested that there was a need for an ombudsman in Sarajevo, and when asked why, he replied that it would then be possible to complain if the buses didn't run on time! This did not however seem to be the most pressing problem there in those days.

But to return to the progression of rights: we are now arriving at the beginning of a formulation of group and cultural rights. Important protocols have been drawn up about subjects such as

lesser-used languages, or minority rights in a society dominated by
one group, and it is against this background that we can revisit the
problem of containing cultural difference, to the extent of encouraging diversity, even in deeply divided societies within a single political entity.

It is perhaps arguable that a polity can only contain one cultural
identity and can thus require conformity to this, although one problem here is that different traditions may not always be compatible.
This is true if we argue – as I would tend to – that not only is difference valuable in a society, but that we can measure the health of a
society by the amount of difference it can contain, without actually
falling apart. It is a mark of the maturity of a society to have such differences without having to mediate them in order to avoid descent
into violence.

One of the dangers of propounding these arguments is that we
tend to think of values – especially those we hold ourselves – as com-
fortable and cosy things. But in a divided society differences can be
quite corrosive and traditions do not always bed in easily with each
other. That is a particular difficulty when part of a culture is defined
by antipathy or opposition to another one. It is an interesting study to
see earlier in this century how much of Irishness was composed of
Anglophobia.

So, traditions may not always be compatible and may even be inim-
icable. Some are hostile, some are perceived to be hostile, some are
intended to be hostile. Much of what passes for tradition in this and
in other countries is of fairly recent origin, created for political and
ideological reasons. Most of what passed for popular Irish history – on
both sides – was the creation of political journalists in the last century.
This is true for what passes for common culture as well, as in the case
of the traditional march which began last year. It is particularly
difficult to deal with, for example, marches which commemorate military victories by one side over another. Where there has been a win-
ner, there will also have been losers; where there are settlers or
colonists, however impressive their struggle, there will be the dispossessed. And those people will take quite a different view of this
struggle and whether it should be celebrated or not.

Several years ago, at the time of the French Bicentennial, when I
found myself in the Vendée on the 14 July, I was struck by the
extremely mixed feelings I encountered there as to whether they
should be celebrating 1789 at all, because that area had really felt the
smack of the terror. While all the fireworks were going off you could

see little crowds at the back waving placards saying 'Vendéens contre le Bicentennial!' The same sorts of questions were raised also in Australia during the bicentennials there. In this case the celebrations were by the population of what they saw as an empty land, but the indigenous Australians had a different poimt of view, as if they were saying: 'We were here for a long time before you were – what about us?'

I was also very struck at a speech given in Dublin a couple of years ago by FW de Klerk, then President of South Africa. Talking about his first meeting with the leader of the African National Congress, Nelson Mandela, he said that for a long time they discussed not politics but what they called the Anglo-Boer War. And the idea that Mandela with his tradition and background should be able to appreciate the triumphs of the Boers which meant defeat by proxy for the black people of South Africa was enough to get them on the same wavelength and get them talking. The binding-up of wounds is particularly difficult in the differential interpretation of history, especially after a long civil war or something akin to that. The problem then is how to celebrate difference without denaturing or destroying it.

I would like now to talk about cultural diversity not just in Northern Ireland but also in a wider framework. My hypothesis is that society is enriched by difference and by range of choice, and that pluralism, openness to change and tolerance of diversity are more likely to provide a basis for mutual trust and the resolution of conflict than insularity and protectiveness. The Lurgan poet George Russell (known as 'Æ', and a contemporary of the young Yeats) wrote a paper called 'Thoughts for a Convention'. This was in 1917 when yet another convention had been assembled to solve the Irish problem. He wrote with a caveat against a majority-imposed culture which would repress all difference, arguing that the ideal to aim at was a diversity of culture and the greatest freedom and variety of thought. He said that the more richness and variety prevailing in a nation, the less likely would be a tyranny of one culture over the rest.

We in Ireland should aim at the freedom of the ancient Athenians whose Pericles said we should listen gladly to the opinions of others, and not turn sour faces on those who disagree with us. We should allow the greatest freedom and cultural respect in Ireland so that the best may triumph by reason of superior beauty and not because the police are relied upon to maintain one culture in a superior position.

This sounds all very laudable until you remember that Athenian culture admitted of slavery! But there it is.

Culture can be looked at in many ways – and I mean more than 'high' culture or the Arts. I mean also identity: the set of values defining a culture or people, which is an amalgam of shared historical experience, political and economic structures, religion, folklore and ethnicity. I have been interested for a long time in exploring whether cultural pluralism is possible in a society, whether it is possible for one political unit to contain several sets of values, and deep conflicts between these. This was caught by Richard Rose in one of the better books on the Northern Ireland question called *Governing Without Consensus*, written in the late 1960s.[2] He said that where the conflict is about deeply-held things like allegiance or identity, no compromise is possible. He called these things the 'great unbargainables'. No consensus was available on these fundamental issues and government without this could only be achieved by integration or assimilation and repression. But the thing to remember about culture is that it changes – it is not static. It is composed of a variety of different factors which themselves change over time. The Ireland of today, North or South, is not the Ireland of previous generations. Change is taking place almost, in many cases, despite the custodians of group and national values. The Ireland of tomorrow will be different again. And so will Britain. And it is within this picture of a dynamic society that one needs to think of cultural diversity. It is interesting to see the extent to which borders are now permeable.

I think, for example, that what brought down the Berlin Wall was the fact that people could look at their television sets and see what was happening on the other side of it. The speed with which information can be transferred across the world makes it extremely difficult for an insular culture to survive without being changed in some way. It is both sad, and interesting, that in our conflict here, people are increasingly fighting enemies who existed decades ago but are quite different now. The unionist perception of the Republic is based on a stereotype from the 1930s which bears no relation to present reality, and we will have to wait for this to ferment away before we can have any real development.

I am not of the view that total assimilation is much of a recipe for dealing with cultural minorities. Melting-pot theory, even in the land of its birth, has been fairly well discredited. It is interesting that countries like Australia, Canada and New Zealand who are setting themselves up as multicultural societies are finding they need to do so in a structured way, providing by charter for the rights and dignities of different groups.

It is possible to maintain difference through economic pluralism, where different groups co-exist separately, coming together only in the market-place, or structural pluralism where the groups are contained in different structures with their own institutions. There will always be a tension between the centralising forces of civism, expressed for example through state control of education, and pluralism, where value systems and mechanisms are controlled by the groups in society. This is a complicated way of saying that it has to be both top-down and bottom-up.

One way of looking at the relationship is to distinguish between the nation as a sort of horizontal network of trust and identity, and the state as a vertical structure of powers. These can come together, as in the idealised nation state, but not often. Other combinations and arrangements are possible. What is clear is that groups can have identity problems. The solidarity of the group is an important support to the individual who can often only realise himself through identification with a group. A group can also of course be a constraint on individual freedom, for example where there is a requirement on the individual to behave according to the group norms. But just as an individual needs to be secure in himself, which is one element in maturity, so also groups, and especially minority groups, need to develop self-confidence. A self-confident group secure in its own values can deal with other groups much more constructively than can a group which is insecure or sees itself as oppressed or undervalued.

Much inter-group or ethnic conflict is, I believe, determined by the self-perception of the groups concerned, by their conception of others and their preconception of others' views of them. Underlying most of these conflicts is a failure of communication, a lack of empathy and understanding, which results in stereotyping and scapegoating, and a basic lack of that trust without which no social, political or other contract is achievable. I see the thing almost as a series of Venn diagrams where the groups overlap so that some have common membership, some have separate membership, with some sharing. Each of those groups needs to have a fairly secure boundary around it in order to preserve sufficient self-confidence to move forward. In relation to the two main communities in Northern Ireland, where you see what Keith Kyle described as the 'overlap' of nationalities, for the unionist population or tradition the boundary of their Venn diagram has to be secure enough to convince them that they will not be sucked against their will into a united Ireland where they will be dominated by people of the other tradition. Equally, the boundary of the nationalist group needs to be secure enough to reassure them that they will not be sucked into some integrated UK or left in a situation where they will form a permanent minority. To ensure this, boundaries have to be permeable so that ideas flow through them, so that there can be communication across and through them and so that the richness of each of the parts can enliven and stimulate the whole.

I would argue too that an individual can exist in more than one cultural milieu at the same time. Most of us do. As a test, consider the sort of accent we use. The purpose of speech is to communicate, and we usually concentrate on what we say rather than how we say it. I would use different speech talking to a fisherman from Killough than I would use giving a lecture in London or Washington. Each of us varies forms of expression in different circumstances. This may be a small detail but it does show that people can grow and occupy three or four bits of overlapping cultural space at the same time, and most of us define ourselves by several overlapping frames of reference.

My argument would be for variety over singleness, for multiculture over monoculture. It may be that we need a group of special, polyvalent people to act as interpreters and I always think of Seamus Heaney's poem in which someone watching a diviner at work asks to have a go. Nothing happens, until the diviner 'nonchalantly grips expectant wrists'. The twig then stirs again. I think these might be the valuable people who can pick up the secret messages on the underground radio stations and relay them to others. The more people we have who are literate in more than one cultural model, the better it might be.

An American academic called John Higham has provided a theoretical rationalisation of this. He talked about a framework for cultural diversity, and said that in contrast to the integrationist model, it will not eliminate ethnic boundaries but neither will it maintain them intact. It will uphold the validity of a common culture to which all individuals have access, while sustaining the efforts of minorities to preserve and enhance their own integrity. In principle, this dual commitment can be met by distinguishing between boundaries and nucleus. No ethnic group under these terms may have the support of a general community in strengthening its boundaries. Whole boundaries are understood to be permeable. Ethnic nuclei are on the other hand respected as enduring centres of social action. The core here involves the sort of values which are required for a settled society, values of respect for law and human rights. What you have in the ethnic nuclei are the differences which make them different and which they can enjoy and celebrate.

I would almost argue that it is a civic duty of diverse groups in society to make their diversity available to other members of society. One of the difficulties in highly stratified or deeply divided societies is the extent to which people cut themselves off from valuable and enriching cultural experiences, ways of looking at life which the other group might have. People should regard it as a civic duty to explain to others why their ways of life are valuable, and to do this in terms which are not threatening. At the present time, with the North Commission on parades sitting, people should really have to explain why marches are important to them, what they mean, to what extent they are an integral part of their tradition, and whether or not they are intended to be threatening, as others claim them to be. In other words I think the Orangemen have a duty to explain to the rest of the world why it is so important to them to march. I think the rest of the world would give them a hearing. In the course of that dialogue, the Orangemen may begin to appreciate why some people do feel threatened by them. Another red rag is the Irish language. Those who insist on promoting this in a certain way should be asked to explain why. It is time for us to try to develop a more open and self-critical society, which can cope with cultural diversity, different allegiances and traditions, without this tearing it apart. This might enable us to replace FSL Lyons'[3] rather bleak conclusion that culture in Ireland can only lead to anarchy, with Roy Foster's[4] more optimistic view of cultural diversity as a means of irrigating the political and social desert.

NOTES

1. Gerard Manley Hopkins, 1877.
2. Richard Rose, *Governing Without Consensus: an Irish Perspective* (Faber, 1971).
3. F.S.L. Lyons, *Culture and Anarchy in Ireland* (Oxford, Clarendon Press, 1979).
4. R.F. Foster, *Modern Ireland 1600–72* (London, Allen Lane, 1988).

CHAIRMAN'S CLOSING REMARKS

Sean Nolan

This conference has been about culture. The late Hermann Goering is usually, though wrongly, given credit for a comment on culture which in its turn is frequently quoted. It was in fact a contemporary of Goering's, the poet Hanns Johst, who said: 'Whenever I hear the word culture, I release the safety catch on my pistol.' A more civilised definition was given by TS Eliot who described culture as 'the whole life of the people'. But we have been accustomed to defining culture in aesthetic and anthropological terms, and I always keep making the point that we forget about the scientific, because 'culture' in scientific terms refers to the act of tilling, of husbandry, of the breeding and rearing of animals. It also refers to the process of growth in a micro-organism in laboratory conditions, so I would want to emphasise that culture is not static but is about growth, that is, it is something which is developing and evolving all the time, so that we do acquire new cultures and new ideas. Perhaps the most all-embracing definition, however, comes from the 1982 UNESCO Conference on Cultural Policies:

> In its widest sense, culture may now be said to be the whole complex of distinctive spiritual, material, intellectual and emotional features which characterises a society or social group. It includes not only the arts and letters but also modes of life, the fundamental rights of the human being, value systems, traditions and habits.

The policy document from the Council of Europe, 'In From the Margins', suggests that the keys to cultural policy are:

◁ promoting cultural identity;
◁ promoting cultural diversity;
◁ promoting creativity;
◁ promoting participation.

As an extension of that policy, Francis Fukuyama, in his book *The End of History and the Last Man*[1] suggests that differences between societies and their social problems manifest themselves at a cultural level, not on the level of states and public policy. If you reflect on who controls society throughout the world today, you would have to say that multinational corporations have a strong influence on how policy is determined.

From what you have heard at this conference, those problems already manifest themselves here and in many other parts of Europe. The task which faces us as we approach the new century will be to identify our problems correctly, and as Julian Huxley remarked, a problem properly identified is a problem half solved. So I think that is the big task. Michael D Higgins, when minister responsible for cultural affairs in the Republic of Ireland (but who is also an academic and poet), made the positive observation that 'when you invest in culture, you are investing in tolerance, you are investing in diversity, and you are investing in creativity and imagination'.

There has been a rich diet of ideas over these past few days which will require some time for digestion; I think that the exchange of responses to the topics raised at this conference would be a fruitful continuation of it.

Thank you all for being here, especially those of you who have come from continental Europe and have made quite a long journey. I hope that we have learned something of our cultures at various levels, and that in spite of our present problems, we will take away a more positive view of the society that we live in.

NOTE

1. F. Fukuyama, *The End of History and the Last Man*, Hamish Hamilton, London, 1992.